Fierce and Furious Critique of How:
"America's Polarizing Dissension" Fuels Its Descent

Wayne Cade

Waytyke Press— Gaithersburg, MD
Paperback ISBN: 979-8-218-52611-5
eBook ISBN: 979-8-3304-7585-8
Library of Congress Control Number: 2024921578
Title: *Fierce and Furious Critique of How: "America's Polarizing Dissension" Fuels its Descent*
Author: Wayne Cade
Digital distribution | 2024
Paperback | 2024

Molesting my Soul
(A Poem)

It appears that I'm living in a country
Where I'm denied equal opportunity
Kept stagnant in my economic stature
Due racism that permeates the culture
Which historically distorts or obliterates
My ability and efforts to assimilate
I don't comport with that experience
As it obscures my legitimate grievance
I'm wrongly denounced for lacking ambition
Oxymoronically resented for my competition
Just an example of molesting my soul!

We're kept marginal and non-competitive
Face advancement policies that are prohibitive
Don't equate my experience with that of others
Because no immigrant here has ever suffered
The inhumane brutality of American slavery
Which was the worst form in global history
Every migrant that came here have all excelled
While my dream was deferred strategically withheld
Day after day I contemplate and plan
The virtuous values on which to stand
Frequently encountering those in opposition
Who're carrier's of obstacles of resistance
Another example of molesting my soul!

Some republicans are impediments to progress
The following are the immediate threats
Senator's: Cruz, Kennedy McConnell, Hawley
Graham, Lee, both Scott's and Grassley
Cornyn, Cassidy, Burr, Hyde-Smith and Ernst
Representatives: McCarthy, Jordan, Boebert,
Ousting them all cannot be done arbitrarily
Only by collaboration in the next primary
It does not matter what the party affiliation
Any replacement will be better for the nation

Removing these members is a step toward
Turning away from trump and going forward
This is why we need to adopt term limits
For both House members and the Senate
Removing big contributions from elections
Which stains the recipients like an infection
Then change the rules of the Supreme Court
After 25 years of service they must depart
Two recent appointees were unqualified
And regrettably they can't be nullified

No more judges with a biased philosophy
Only those aspiring to interpret litigiously
Institutions that function in an archaic way
Needs an infusion of new ideas today
Stop the influence peddlers called lobbyists
Due to their efforts, political bribery persists
The GOP legislature is indelibly stained
For dereliction of duty and a need to change
The lies of a former president they embrace
While denying the truth what a disgrace
Choosing to prop up and embolden the liar

Is leading the party to an unquenchable fire
Most are now predisposed to the abdication
Of their vows and commitment to the nation
Perpetuating crimes against common decency
Has for them become a standing tendency
Many provable lies are met by their silence
Price of admission to their party is defiance
Conservatives have gotten really bold
In their blind pursuit of power and control
They never tire in molesting our soul

Preface

Within this book, many of the subsequent conclusions I've drawn are capable of unraveling for the reader a host of misinformed or simply false statements and assumptions that's being propagated by a major political party despite incontrovertible evidence to the contrary. Many sources of this negativity occupy political offices and influential positions representing a clear and present danger that undermines and threatens democracy and unfortunately, we've placed our power in the hands of those who've abdicated all morality and neglect us. And since we've tolerated their nonsense for so long, they've become confident and comfortable with our acquiescence and will never change so we must change, starting with voting them out and with our vote, only empower those who look to empower us. With an uncompromising devotion to a higher standard in the pursuit of knowledge, wisdom, understanding and discernment the questions raised within these pages are written with the intent of bringing awareness and to encourage a change to the politics we've tolerated for so long.

The world is changing all around us and unfortunately too many low information Americans, void of analytical verification skills are influenced by false accusations leveled against the Democratic party which are simply projections and admissions of the faults and shortcomings of the Republican party. These knowledge-deprived fellow citizens aligned themselves with Maga and boarded the accelerating Republicans train to polarization and willfully have chosen to be handcuffed to antiquated and obsolete beliefs propagated by delusional self-serving men with their own unquenchable thirst for power and control.

This style of politics currently reflected in the indisputable crippling incapacity of congressional republicans to produce legislation beneficial to the masses instead of just for corporations is a disastrous detriment to democracy and should be a rallying cry to voters to reject and remove such remnants from their offices.

The foundation of our democracy has been under attack by brazen partisans with a corrupt intent to replace it with fascism. In defense and preservation of our democratic principles the entire Maga movement that's clearly incompatible with the fundamental principles of democracy must be opposed. I am not telling anyone how to cast their vote but I can assure you that Maga's efforts will fail and democracy will prevail if voters in 2024 strongly consider democrat down the ballot because failing to do so ensures the gradual transition to fascism in America. These dangerous incompatible obstacles to democracy must be met with our strongest dissent and resistance.

Chapter 1

Since the formation of what's oxymoronically referred to as the United States the country has acquired and maintained a position of global, economic and military dominance. A position it could never have achieved or maintained without the false promise of freedom to Black slaves in order to gain their support against the British during the Revolutionary War. This baseless promise premised on the colonist's desire for independence from the British crown was never intended to be kept. After the war, America reneged on this promise and Blacks found their experiences of inhumane oppressive acts worse than before the war. The Revolutionary War was not commissioned with the objective of altering Black people's status, instead it became the catalyst for the gradual ascension to unequaled economic heights for the newly formed capitalistic democratic nation. America's victory in the war is celebrated every year on the 4th of July and for Blacks, it's the "4th of you lie." Following the war three coequal branches of government was established and intended as a safeguard from dominance and control by either of the three individual branches.

For nearly 250 years, despite various forms of internal conflict the country with both clarity and determination has effectively managed to maintain its system of government. Two ensuing conflicts, the War 1812 and the Civil War had the potential to dismantle the established form of government and these two assaults could easily have eroded the democratic ideals along with the capitalistic system of government. They represented the greatest threats to the nation until the Civil Rights struggles to the mid-20th century and the J6th event of this 21st century where we are faced with the prospect of a criminal former president again being nominated by his party for the office he once occupied and totally disgraced.

A brief glimpse of a small part of our history is the conduit through which the formation of my writing is derived. To my casual observers reading this book the information within is not intended to offend any individual and it's based on a combination of public reports and expressions of my own sentiments based on those reports. Throughout this book when referring to the former president his name is deliberately not capitalized because of my personal disdain for crooks. My hope is that the context of this information will fuel debate, educate and empower as well as inspire an unwavering pursuit of corroborating research on the Republican purveyors of negativity.

There's been a failure of the general public to recognize the corruption and greed of many corporate America and governmental structures whose collateral expense of operating imperils the masses and hopefully this information will spur awareness and prompt the pursuit of appropriate and revitalizing remedies for the masses who are adversarially impacted by the far-reaching tentacles of those structures. Essentially a decisive and aggressive stance must be adopted towards our identified adversaries whose unequivocal hostilities against our democracy have already been articulated and disseminated. The deception and conspiracy theories of both trump and House Republicans has captivated and influenced a sizable segment of society and exemplifies the need for reform in our political arena.

The 1954 Brown v. Board of Education Supreme Court (SCOTUS) decision is where I'll begin my journey into exploring the likely causes for America's gradual descent from its lofty height as a global power. The Brown case was derived from five separate school segregation petitions in SC, VA, Kansas, Delaware and DC. The name of the case came from assistant Pastor Oliver Brown a Topeka, Kansas resident who in 1950 was prevented from enrolling his daughter in a public school. The school was only a few blocks from her home but because of the refusal to allow her enrollment she had a two hour commute via bus and car to a segregated school. Oliver Brown went to the local NAACP where at least a dozen petitions were pending and the Brown name became the reference for the collective body of five petitions selected to present their argument before the court.

The argument eventually led to the unanimous 1954 SCOTUS decision effectively, at least on paper, ending state sanctioned segregation of public schools which had been operating on the separate but equal precedent established by the same court 60 years earlier. Nationwide adherence to the court's ruling wasn't immediate as there were school districts that deliberately closed for multiple years in an effort to curtail the implementation of desegregation rather than integrate as ordered by the court. All southern states and their respective representative members of Congress adopted what's animously known as the Southern Manifesto drafted by SC senator Strom Thurmond which declared that the Brown decision would be resisted by any and all means. However the legal victory represented in the Brown decision became the catalyst for desegregation in many other areas such as the historically significant (1964) civil rights act and public accommodation, (1968) fair housing act, (1965) voting rights act which all have a continuing impact today. But because of the structural inequalities and the inherent moral decay of our country each of these victories were rebuffed and met with strong resistance, especially in the southern states.

These controversial adjudicated changes interrupted the way of life for the majority population who indulged in domestic terrorism against minorities and imposed Jim Crow laws that prevented access to the practical and material benefits of citizenship for what was perceived by them to be a subhuman population. In the struggle for civil rights the culmination of our efforts were reflected in the dissipation of segregation and the adoption of integration in the mid-1960s which was in a way detrimental to the Black community because many Black owned businesses sold to foreigners and fled the Black community for suburban areas.

By the 1980s after close examination of the condition and the wreckage of the nation, the relocated Black suburbanites realized they had integrated into a burning house. The wreckage appeared to be paramount not just in their communities but in both political parties as well. But one would find it more prevalent in the Republican party whose elusive bankruptcy of action does not match their appealing words spoken as candidates for office.

When these charlatan candidates are running for office, they make it their business to visit areas where excluded Americans reside in places of poverty, pain and indignities then they make promises only to get into office and deny us. Without any policy platform, during voting season they eagerly embark on these tours of deception referred to as campaigns which are filled with buzz words to attract the vote of their constituents solely for the purpose of gaining or remaining in office where they go on to protect donor interests and practice their self-serving agendas while avoiding or rarely engaging in legislation beneficial to their constituents. This is indicative of the divisive culture masquerading as an inclusive one that's being fostered by this new Maga Republican party that promotes inherently radical racial ideology which now permeates throughout our society.

With little or no representation in their state government or the federal congressional body the minority population adopted the method of nonviolence to navigate through conflicts and strongly believed that the court and congress were the only venues where unfair practices could be challenged. Decades before the Brown decision, as an agent of political and personal change, the NAACP had a number of successes breaking the barrier of segregation on the collegiate educational level beginning in the 1930s but the most significant was Brown vs Board of Education.

Chapter 2

During the social justice campaigns of 2022 the Black population discovered that what they once believed to be a friend in the supreme court and the legislative branch of the federal government had become a foe which no longer made rulings or crafted policy to benefit the oppressed or the marginalized and even appeared to have become antagonistic impediments to the progress of any sector of our society except for themselves and corporations. This undoubtedly is apparent in 2023 where we find both congress and the courts have been infiltrated by members whose socially polarizing agenda and cultural biases strongly mirror the positions of Civil Rights era segregationists. A manipulative strategy has been adopted by a number of Justices and congressmen who are prompted and propelled to actively resist or abort any petitions and legislation that will equally or heavily favor the minority population. Here's a few examples:

1) Many state legislatures across the country and courts have ruled affirmative action in college admissions is no longer needed for minorities. In 2023 the super conservative majority supreme court heard arguments and decided to end the practice nationally as it relates to minority admissions but they left intact preferences for donors, employees' family members and legacy admissions which essentially is affirmative action

for Whites. One must realize that decisions like this must be met with an elevated degree of skepticism because they're simultaneously based on some kind of resentment or detachment coupled with a smothering degree ignorance.

2) Early on in the Covid-19 pandemic our country's efforts to find a cure were genuine and intense until scientists reported that minorities were disproportionately affected and likely to die from the virus. Following that report the urgency of the trump administration to find a cure, quickly dissipated and the shameful manifestation of a malignant and lethal hate of Blacks was being expressed by trump's new wavering policy for fighting the virus. Efforts by the CDC (Center for Disease Control) to develop a vaccine and our collaboration with the WHO (World Health Organization) as well as some private research efforts were aborted, a sudden shortage of masks/ppe and the harvesting of ventilators by the administration after trump realized that Blacks were disproportionately affected.

3) Joe Biden signed an executive order canceling a modest portion of student debt which will equally benefit both minority and White students. Republican opposition to the order prompted petitions to the courts and after successful appeals in the lower courts the SCOTUS reversed Biden's executive order.

To further illustrate how government interference in issues that favors minorities, again I refer to Brown v. Board of Education and the delayed implementation of that decision. One of the deciding justices employing a dilatory tactic amended the language of the text, removing the word "forthwith" to include the words "with all due speed." This difference in the text provided the states opposing the decision, the leeway necessary to indefinitely delay immediate implementation of the SCOTUS decision. Since our arrival in this country we've been the constant victims of government sponsored and church sanctioned cruelties and injustices similar to those that later influenced South Africa's system of apartheid and the German brutality during the Holocaust.

I can assure you without contradiction that the phenomenon of governmental or judicial interference and disruption of minority affairs in this nation are intricate parts of the foundational elements in the formation of the country. Being socially deprived and economically denied is what bred our discontent with the unjust treatment we've experienced here as a people since our arrival and has been clearly illustrated by the numerous intermittent rebellions in the formative years of the nation and continuing through the protest years of the 60s and 70s.

In contrast the British war against the American colonists known as the Revolutionary War was fought to abolish the colonists' own slavery to Britain while they hypocritically imposed brutal slavery on Africans. For nearly two and a half centuries in spite of her own revolting barbarity and shameless hypocrisy, the US boasts of her independence every 4th of July while it still overtly, covertly and aggressively fights against the independence, equality and the improvement of the condition of its ex-slaves.

The promotion of the American dream being attainable for all has always been a nebulous concept for the Black man who since his arrival here has had a predestined role as slaves. It's past time for the development of a coalition of confrontation against the policies and the philosophies of trump and the MAGA cult which wants to simultaneously introduce a level of suffering with the most deleterious impact on the Black community. The rhetoric of trump is inconsistent with his actions and policies, triggering my cry for confrontation against his old-time vision for the Maga cult and remind him that those bad old days will never be replicated again in America. We must ensure that the racist ghosts driving trump's efforts to exhume Jim Crow from the grave, are futile and will never come to fruition to further unravel the civic fabric of the nation. We must never lose our grip on the slippery uphill climb to equality despite alarming government proposed reductions in social programs that uplift people while increasing the military budget even in times of peace.

As a people we've fought for inclusion and have had numerous small victories of which a number have been or are currently being undermined by the Court's. In essence the sought-after inclusion has been an illusion as there's been only a slight measurable difference for us in terms of freedom, justice and equality since the Revolutionary War until now. Paradoxically we are told to be non-violent and passive in our struggle for justice and equality instead of adopting the European model employed during the Revolutionary War.

Fast forward to 1865, following the Civil War. The Statue of Liberty was commissioned to be built by a Frenchman named de Laboulaye. The original idea and intent of the statue was for the celebration of the ending of the Civil War and the ending of slavery in America.

The original artistic design for the statue conceived by de Laboulaye was to depict a Black woman breaking the bonds of slavery with the broken shackles at her feet. Several of the original models are housed in the basement of the NY City Museum (5th Ave and 106th St). One can find additional corroborating evidence at the French Cultural Center (5th Ave and 82nd Street) which has a special edition of the magazine "France" in which the real story is told and original models are illustrated. In the final analysis the deliberate refusal to ascribe any recognition whatsoever, to the originally intended Black representation of the symbol of America, has been sponsored and promoted by the government to point where to this day Americans erroneously believe that the emergence of the statue was intended to welcome immigrants to a land of liberty.

The preceding points are indicative of the longstanding and ongoing governmental efforts to prevent progress for and recognition of the minority population. And because of widespread inherent racism deeply embedded in the fabric of the nation. These efforts persist today, as republican congressmen, harboring their artificial concerns, continue to resist calls for DC statehood and in an artificial fashion adversarially inserts itself in the affairs of the minority controlled local government in DC. Yet they lack any concern for identically important domestic issues in their own districts such as poverty, hunger and racism.

There is little space for one whose conscience urges them to a particular course of action but are forced to take another when the dynamics of a situation is perceived as an obstacle or an impediment. The ramifications of this type of reversal is that passivity rarely gets one to their desired destination when courage is abandoned and in the words of James Baldwin "not everything that is faced can be changed but nothing can be changed until it is faced." Over the years we've had Black leaders who actively engaged in the struggle for justice and improvement of the minority condition in this Country each with varying degrees of success. We've had:

Frederick Douglas
Marcus Garvey
Booker T Washington
W E B Dubois
Nat Turner
Medgar Evers
Martin Luther King
Bayard Rustin
Shirley Chisholm
Asa Phillips Randolph
Thurgood Marshall
Fannie Lou Hamer
Malcolm X
Fred Hampton

These among a host of others all fought for the equitability of opportunity for the Black race requiring us being lifted from a horizontal to a vertical social position and the inclusion of us experiencing equality as an everyday reality and not just an ideal or a concept described in the nation's founding documents.

Most of us only know the sanitized version of these activist icons who today would all be categorized on the political spectrum as leftists or progressives. An untold number of them were amenable to the fomenting of rebellions and refused to be bound by any laws established without their representation or voice. A number of our prominent activists were assassinated or exiled when their radical plans, to organize a radical political force and empower the poor, were exposed. On the national stage Malcolm and King made their appeals to transform the nation's soul and open opportunities for people, not for themselves, nor their friends, or the highest corporate bidder.

There was not a scent of extortion, greed or self-gratification in their inclusivity movements only a determination to erase the nation's birth defects of racism and segregation. They fought to counter and reduce in this country the historical oppression of Black people as a class issue instead of simply a race issue as inferred in the constitution. I must include Fred Hampton as his movement shared the aspirations of Malcolm and Martin but due to his execution by police, he never reached the national stage. Had he not been killed by Chicago police while asleep in his bed, he eventually would have been propelled onto the national scene.

Fortunately for the baked in biased system of our government, these leaders cited above were never able to collaborate as most were from different generational eras and in the case of King and Malcolm who appeared to agree on the objective but were adverse to each other's approach. Based on the virtuous values ascribed to these leaders had we been afforded the simultaneous presence and collective efforts of these activists I believe equality for the minority would have been gained long ago.

These activists discovered that the lack of consistent media attention and the absence of political will to deal with rising poverty added to the alienation and isolation of the poor, especially Blacks. Propelled by their widespread apathy and disgust of the political and governmental structures of the nation with enthusiasm they fought for the revitalization of an excluded and economically demoralized people. Each in their own way fought against the remnants of bigotry and White supremacy in order to make meaningful changes by challenging homogenization over diversity, inequality over equity and exclusion over inclusion because they knew that evil triumphs only when good men do nothing. It's now our turn to ignite our inner fires of commitment, determination and idealism, because depending on the brilliance of those flames, future generations will either look back with gratitude at our strength or they will suffer the consequences of our weakness.

Chapter 3

When it comes to the descendants of ex-slaves, American politics has been afflicted by compassion fatigue which is why the minority has to be inspired and empowered to fight for ourselves. And what we must clearly and pragmatically understand is that since the founding of our country, regardless of the lofty ideas engraved on paper such as, the Constitution or the Declaration of Independence, the inherent aversion of most White towards Blacks remains unchanged. Our emotionalized sentimentality to the expressed ideas of the aforementioned documents has never changed the nature of Blacks in this country and any intelligent and logical study or scrutinization of our history will reveal this.

Across racial lines there is agreement that what kills or retards the human spirit and undermines the discipline of hard work is the poor remaining too dependent on the government. I must point out that just as there has been many positive activists among our people we've regretfully had and still have some perpetrators, sellouts, self-haters and phonies who regularly manifest a blatant contempt for Blacks like Jesse Lee (Jumbo Sambo) Peterson, Candace Owens (Coon Queen) and Larry Elder whose buffoonery tells White people that the dangerous resurgence of White supremacy is okay. And the sad part is that these self-emasculated sellouts are not categorized or compartmentalized by Whites differently than other Blacks.

They seemingly have an equal disdain and hatred for Blacks as Whites do which they seek to monetize and are impediments to the efforts of those looking to truly uplift the minority. Some have established broad platforms from which to spew their deception, attempt to repel legitimate criticism of corruption and play the projection game of portraying themselves as reformers but are actually stand-ins for the antagonistic racists. To the delight of the Whites, their tolerance and acceptance of the corruption which excuses the wrongdoing of racists and it undermines the message of Black ability and self-reliance. Most of them use their platform to access corporate leaders to make deals for themselves and they're quick to criticize anyone focused on developing quality institutions or leaders for Black Americans. They fail to recognize that the tough on crime policies adopted and implemented by Congress applies only to Blacks while it ignores the corporate crimes White Americans engage in. Most remain silent on biased disparities in punishment for crimes that accounts for over-representation of Blacks in prison and contributes to the diminishment of the Black family. They've abandoned the fundamental premise of Black leadership in favor of something weaker, morally uncertain and counterproductive.

Decades ago two individuals who I like to think have transcended their earlier shortcomings, would be examples corroborating my assertions: After King's death Jesse Jackson became the media's one stop shopping for a comment on any issues affecting Black

America and he held the mythical post of President of Black America. Following his two unsuccessful bids for President (1984 and 1988) Jesse Jackson positioned himself to hold political posts in Chicago (hometown of PUSH or his native state SC) from where he could have affected broader change for Black Americans but he declined to run for state office.

Consequently he was not involved in passing any laws improving schools or any other key issues facing Black America. He did manage to enrich himself in the 1980s when he boycotted Budweiser with his Bud's a Dud campaign which culminated into a multi-million-dollar beer distribution center for two of his sons.

When Jackson was later caught in a sex scandal involving one of his aides, Al Sharpton aggressively pushed to succeed Jackson with his call for a new generation of leadership. Sharpton ran for President in 2004 and took the model for Black politics to a new low when he took 200K from Roger Stone to finance his failing campaign. The only time Stone showed an interest in Black politics was when he joined the effort to block the recount of the Black vote in Dade County, FL to protect George Bush's victory in the 2000 election.

In 1983, Sharpton secretly gave the FBI information on Black leaders in NY City and in 2005 he took money from LoanMax in exchange for luring poor Black people into its web. The LoanMax fiasco was cited as proof that Sharpton's professed concern for the poor was a charade. In the past both Jackson and Sharpton staged phony protests marches for money. I don't know of any recent ethical or moral shortcomings by either man and since those earlier indiscretions, their histories strongly indicate that they've reformed.

If history teaches you nothing else hopefully you've learned that there's always a Judas to be found among us. To name a few Judas's in this 21st century who have broad far-reaching political platforms that reach sizable audiences from which they constantly spew their pessimistic positions and opinions on matters related to Black advancement we have: Rep. Byron Donalds, Sen. Tim Scott, and a host of others too numerous to name here.

I must clarify that throughout this book my reference to minorities is exclusively talking about Black people while at times it's used interchangeably and includes other groups. This country as a whole has engaged in economic inequality and genocidal racial violence for the majority of its history. But a new legislated strategy has been introduced which now includes mental and economic genocide in which the minority is relegated to a permanent underclass status. Many groups such as the Women's Rights, LGBTQ and Hispanics through convenient consolidation efforts with Black activists have all credited the Civil Rights movement with advancing their causes and have permanently adopted the Civil Rights approach as a model for achieving those groups respective aspirations. There has been a conscious effort, masked in the spirit of cooperation and compromise, to migrate other marginalized groups (mainly immigrants and LGBTQ) issues into our activism resulting in the co-opting of our struggle and becoming a hindrance to our progress.

By aligning these other groups concerns with our own their issues became amplified more than our own and when attention from the government was garnered our issues are unaddressed and relegated to the bottom while these other groups wind up benefitting at our expense. This list includes Jews as well and most of all other immigrant groups in the country. None of them ever experienced antebellum slavery, or Jim Crow, or horrible lynchings, or the brutality of the Civil Rights struggle or the suppressive assaults on the Black Power movement yet they all quickly learned how to capitalize on the term minority. While these groups experience some successes because of their superficial alliance with our struggle but seldom if ever do they stand in alliance with us against the Court's undermining of the legislated gains of the Civil Rights era for the Black minority which includes voting rights and affirmative action.

Our remedy has to be a total rejection of alliances with these groups because unless it's separately addressed, we'll never flourish in America's democracy. Our continued suffering will eventually spur an increasing awareness among the new generation who will adopt a more radical form of protest fermenting into a total rebellion, if they're ignored and denied. As a group, it seems that when we raise our issues and recount the cruelty of our colonization and exploitation that we passed through as a race everyone wants us to let bygones be bygones. Historically we've been the only group asked to do this. Today, America's struggle with the British Empire is still memorialized on the 4th of July, Russia commemorates her struggle with Germany, China never lets her people forget trials and tribulations in their struggle for sovereignty and to this day the Jews will hunt down any affiliated sponsor of their Holocaust. In relation to our nation's receptivity and response to our grievances, we've always been advised to let what happened in the past remain in the past and to absorb and assimilate into a way of life that was never designed or intended for us.

The Jews are thought to have had a long relationship with the Black community in this country due to common historic levels of oppression both groups experienced. The Jews tolerant intermingling with us was self-serving and eventually any perceived solidarity with Blacks was strategically abandoned for social and economic advancement of the Jews. This fact alone substantiates any perceived revulsion Blacks may have towards Jews and clearly demonstrates the historical pattern of Black interactions with all other European groups. Wherever one mentions Jews, the Jewish radar is activated in search of anything that can be construed as antisemitic. One must be made aware that Jewish references to antisemitism is a misused term erroneously ascribed to the misguided Ashkenazi Zionist converts to Judaism. The term Semite has no specific reference to a particular people rather it is a denotation of various biblical or historic languages.

The oppressive Zionists occupiers and their descendants conveniently employ the word antisemite to garner sympathy and support for their continued inhumane disenfranchisement of the Palestinian people. There are multiple groups of Jewish people, the Sephardic who participated and profited from the Atlantic slave trade, the Ashkenazi Jews who were the recipients of German brutality during the Holocaust and the Mizrahi who're believed to be the first Jewish occupants of Middle East and African territories.

The sad story is that today 90% of the global Jewish population have no historical or genetic connection to the Jews of the Bible. This group is known as Ashkenazi Jews who were descendants of the eastern European Khazar people who converted to Judaism around 740 AD. This is a well-known fact among the Ashkenazi's since 1700 AD and to this day it's still disguised and ignored among themselves.

During the era of the slave trade almost every aspect of European maritime commerce was in the control of Sephardic Jews except for the sailing of the ships to and from ports. Jewish cartography as well as Jewish financial aid enabled several of Christopher Columbus voyages. The point of this brings us to an unpopular issue that's not presented in any history of the Jewish people. Jews were major participants in the genocide of Native Americans and were major participants in the greatest human tragedy history knows, the transatlantic trade in Africans as slaves.

There's one Jewish author, Joseph Jacobs, who chronicles the Jewish contributions to the flourishing African slave trade and the inescapable conclusion that Jews had a large and profitable role in New World genocide and slavery. This is not meant to suggest that Jews were solely responsible for the initiation and maintenance of the slave trade but one needs to consider how ineffective those voyages would have been without Jewish participation. Furthermore, the Ashkenazi Jewish claim of a homeland in Palestine is absurd. As I mentioned earlier, they were converts to Judaism with no genetic or historical connection to Palestine at all. In the early 20th century around the end of WWI, Arabs,

Christians and a number of Jews lived peacefully in Palestine but this harmony was disrupted when Zionists began flooding Palestine after WWII.

After the Jewish incursion into Palestine, the Zionists reneged on a UN suggested two state solution and beginning in 1947 until the present day these Zionists have an aversion to Arabs similar to the Nazis against Jews and have been displacing and killing Palestinians in order to colonize, occupy and claim Arab land. I must note for the record that the genuine Jewish people are not the Palestinians problem, it's the Zionist sect with its Maga like cultic attraction of a large segment of Jews that is responsible for the disruptive genocidal attacks against Palestinians.

The origin of present day illegal Jewish occupation and constant illegal new settlement building in Palestine is a consequence of what's known as the 1917 Balfour Declaration which in its historical context resulted in the significant upheaval of Palestinian life as known today. This Declaration made by Europeans about a non-European territory disregarded wishes and presence of native majority population in a manner like the 1885 Berlin Conference did in Africa. The 67-word declaration is regarded as one of the most contested and controversial documents in the modern history of the Arab world. Its aim was to establish a Jewish state in Palestine and was the catalyst that culminated into the 1948 ethnic cleansing of Palestinians which continues to this day.

I urge the readers to review the Balfour Declaration for yourself, it's just 67 words. This Jewish claim to Palestine is as silly as a group of Native Americans converting to Catholicism and then demanding that a piece of the Vatican be designated as their homeland.

The present day state of Israel was established by deception, made possible by the combination of Jewish influence in the US mass media and international finance. The dominant Jewish control of US mass media prominently describes Palestinian actions as massacres, atrocities and slaughter but when referencing Israel's intrusive colonial occupation or its dominance and barbaric aggression against Palestinians, it's always justified as preserving life and liberty. In this long running conflict Israel adamantly refers to Hamas as terrorists rather than militants which is a more accurate description because the world understands a militant but despises a terrorist. The flagrant contradictive hypocrisy of western media's narratives and discourse on the matter must be met with skepticism because rarely if at all does it use words like, mass atrocities, or massacre of refugees, when referencing Israeli actions and it ignores the apartheid like conditions Israel imposes on the Palestinians which fomented the brewing ground for the birth of Hamas.

Because of our strategic alliance with Israel despite issues we may have with illegal settlements and open-air prisons the Palestinians are living in, Israel is by far the largest recipient of no strings attached US aid (welfare) which includes an annual $3.8 Billion ($10 million a day) which was established as a condition of the Egypt/Israel peace agreement. That aid finances Israel's missile defense systems and affords them the strongest and most capable military in the region. Inadvertently, our aid funds Israel's incremental increase in atrocities against Palestinians, frequently resulting in the deaths of innocent women and children, yet America is adverse to providing school lunches to its own children and healthcare to its own citizens.

By comparison, according to antagonistic Republican congressmen claims, US Aid to Ukraine is allegedly funding salaries and social programs for Ukrainians but the same Congressmen selectively overlook the fact that some of our Israeli aid is used for those same purposes as well as for free health care and their military's genocidal push in Palestine. Don't get mad, prove me wrong. The 1947 contract negotiated by the United Nations to create Israel was opposed by Yosemite Dushinsky the chief rabbi in Israel at that time who stated at the UN council meeting, "I object to the creation of an Israeli state in any part of Palestine."

But the contract was affirmed due to the following reasons: heavy Zionist influence over the UN council, deliberate deception, blatant propaganda, influence, money and it excluded both Arab or Palestinian representation. In regards to the latter, it mirrored the 1885 Berlin Conference that formally colonized and partitioned out Africa among Europeans without any African representation. The solution to the Arab Israeli predicament to this day has been unfounded but apparently short of a two state nation there's no hope for a lasting peace in Palestine. The purpose of this information hopefully will afford a better understanding of why the Arab Israeli conflict developed and why a solution to Palestinian predicament must be diplomatically fostered.

Since 1947, Israel has rejected over 100 UN proposed truces opting to maintain the illegal occupation which has evolved into the current conditions Palestinians are forced to live under. Conditions that are horrifically inhumane and as bad if not worse than the former Apartheid in South Africa. The Global and US media companies skewed framing of the conflict contributes to the many inaccurate stories regularly aired about the problems and conditions there. The inexplicit and biased reporting of CNN favors Israel and garners sympathetic international support for Israel while depicting the Palestinians as terrorists.

The Hamas attack and the killing of civilians that preceded the current war must be opposed and condemned as well as Israel's atrocious response which has so far killed as many as 9,000 women and children. Do not mistake my criticism of Israeli occupation of Palestine as antisemitic. I am against the political and diplomatic cover being afforded to Israel by the US, UK and many European countries which equates to complicit support of Israeli crimes against humanity.

As stated before, the Hamas October attack against Israeli civilians must be strongly condemned and opposed but that attack affords no justification for Israel's barbarism for the bombing of innocent Palestinian women and children. The Zionist Israeli government's refusal to adopt a two state solution to end the conflict counters its claim to be a lone democracy in a hostile Arab world and declares its actions against Palestinians are necessary for survival.

The Zionist Israeli government represents an ideal which misconstrues what Judaism means and deceptively shrouded itself in the cloak of Judaism effectively commandeering the global sympathy. The Zionists, who due to their enduring the Holocaust while the world sat silent, utilizes the resulting sympathy to justify endless rivers of the bloodshed of Arabs. The current Zionist's leader Netanyahu will not limit his brutality to just Arabs as he is known to have created the climate resulting in the assassination of former Israeli PM Yitzhak Rabin in 1995. Rabin was on the brink of achieving a two-state solution with Palestinians which the Zionists fervently opposed.

Parenthetically, I hope my readers don't conflate my anti-Zionist sentiments with antisemitism. But Netanyahu was the face of the opposition that resulted in the massive Israeli protests culminating in Rabin's death and he then masterfully channeled the subsequent outrage into his own rise to power. As most of the demonstration protests occurred outside of PM Rabin's apartment, Rabin responded with his own rally where afterwards he was killed by a right wing nut and the immediate response of the rally goers was "BB (Netanyahu) is a murderer."

To this day, Zionists perpetuate the hate that's developing around the world and when convenient are the personification of the same antisemitism that they like to accuse others of. Israel's prevention of Palestinian access to water, food, fuel, medical supplies and electricity in addition to the constant bombing of areas where no known combatants are has been verified and should warrant an immediate freeze of US funding ($10 million a day). Our financing of the Zionist barbarity that Palestinians have been suffering from and subjected to since Israel's occupation of the region must cease at least until peace can be found. Imagine being a homeowner for many years with the entire mortgage paid in full then one day someone knocks on your door and takes possession of your home then relegate you and your family to the backyard. This hypothetically is what Israel actually has done and continues to do to the Palestinians.

Chapter 4

There's a troubling omen brewing for the future of politics in this country. Inspired by Mussolini and heavily influence by Hitler. trump with the power of the presidency in 2024, can singlehandedly accelerate the emergence of the face of fascism and catastrophic change in America. His capitalization on the support of his voter base and the absolute fear of that voter base by Republican congressmen has gained him unwarranted admiration among almost 1/3 of US voters which equals the amount of support Hitler had prior to his takeover of Germany. One of trump's advisors Steve Bannon was an advisor for Brazilian president Bolsonoro who in in 2022 lost his bid for reelection and attempted to remain in office by inspiring a January 6th like protest in Brazil. This same Bolsonoro was at the White House, meeting with trump on January 5th one day before the insurrection here. I don't propose to know what they discussed but with both being desperate to remain in office and both being knowledgeable of coups as tactic to retain power inferences can be made that was among their topics of discussion.

Former Italian leader Mussolini's takeover of Italy is what trump aspires to do in this country. He has transformed the GOP into an autocratic party which allowed the rise of total nut cases like Marjorie Greene (who couldn't formulate a policy for any issue if her life depended on it) from the fringes of the party into leadership positions. For 4 years the country was led by a man who openly parrots fascist narratives, ignored addressing the issue of inequality, knowingly gave his voters false economic perceptions, cozies up with crooked White supremacist groups and used the armed forces and his own militarized police to quash anti-fascist protest movements.

We are living through a global Renaissance of mass nonviolent protests because more people are realizing that trump's pursuit of authoritarianism is a scam, whose goal is to get people to act against their interests, to get people to vote for someone who will strip their rights away, who'll plunder the economy and totally ravage our country with corruption. The Maga adherents view Black equality as oppressive and are on an immoral crusade with a hidden objective of reestablishing Jim Crow throughout the country. Many are representative of an assaulting regiment against our democracy and the majority of them out of their own ignorance fail to perceive that eventually the same Maga movement which they now blindly support will victimize them also.

From the vantage point of the oval office in 2024, trump, with a determined methodical approach, will resume the implementation of his demise of American Democracy which was interrupted only by his 2020 defeat. The gradual loss of the norms of the constitution and its associative liberties, increases exponentially with a trump victory because he already has total control and influence over Republican led state legislatures, Capitol Hill republicans and will heavily rely on a biased judiciary bending in his favor. With J6th as the forerunner, the necessity has arisen for us to accept or reject the poisonous conflict which trump is ultimately driving the nation towards.

A democracy requires some level of facts to operate. Authoritarianism needs propaganda more than violence to maintain its grip on power because it does not survive in truthful environments. In our country there's been an increase in ultranationalism (overwhelming loyalty to a perverted vision of the country often laced with bigotry and racism) whose adherents have aspirations to gain total control and take the country back to pre-civil rights America. Ultranationalism can quickly become authoritarianism. Most of its adherents claim that the role of slavery and race does not change anything about understanding the birth and development of the country. Total nonsense! If you consider the events on January 6th, you'd find that it substantiates my assertion on the goals of Ultranationalism.

The motivation of those insurrectionists can be described as greed and for the preservation of White supremacists' ideals over a minority population. If their greed goes unsatisfied, they become prone to frequent fits of rage and then anger develops triggering bitterness and consuming them with desires for revenge. They're easily set off by minor provocations where their reason and judgement becomes overpowered by their temper subsequently resulting in the carrying of grudges for prolonged periods, refusing to forgive, speaking harshly and acting impulsively based on their bitterness. Since the 2020 election, trump with his lies has cast the political arena into a vast darkness but daylight and truth are on the horizon which eliminates the dark forces. Were one to analyze trump's antics and his futile complaints following the 2020 election conclusions could correctly be made that the former president was playing the victim and widely broadcasting erroneous grievances with the hope gaining sympathy from supporters. To some degree it has been an effective strategy as he's still supported by a majority of republican voters. His wallowing in negativity, excessively lamenting over losing an election and resorting to criminal mischief in an attempt to reverse that loss should clearly reveal that he's unqualified to ever lead the country again or be elected to any public office.

Based on recent statistics on extremism only 13% of those charged in the insurrection were formal members of militant groups. The remaining 87% were typical trump supporters and independent far right extremist. In essence most of those who breached the capital were just regular republicans who by their actions that day demonstrated their susceptibility to being converted to ultranationalism.

The overall trajectory of the far-right movement in the US has been massive growth exacerbated by the influence of a failed criminal former president who has captured an audience and is directing this drama for what seemingly can be a TV show titled "The Big Lie" that's playing out on the world stage instead of a TV set. Unlike any other TV show all supporting cast members perform for free and only the star of the show (trump) is getting paid through donations he's grifting from his followers. The 2024 election will determine if there will be a sequel to trump's drama and voters must totally reject the possibility of a sequel to that madness.

Despite immense factual discrepancies trump's message still attracts racist sympathizers, contaminates police forces across the country, attracts and influences active and former military veterans and is rising through the ranks of state legislatures as well as Congress. White supremacy, which has run through the course of the nation's history has, with the aid of trump, commandeered the platform of the Republican party, which now strategically aspires to transform the government into a White supremacy affiliate. With coddling and motivation from trump, members of White supremacist groups have moved from operating in the fringes to the forefront of society and have in many instances managed to gain control and influence in the Senate, the HOR (House of Representatives) Governor's mansions, state legislatures, school boards and a number of local and state governmental bodies throughout the nation.

The pattern trump is following to seize power is identical to that of Hitler with White supremacy as the backbone and in the forefront. Late in the 19th century (around 1885) trump's grandfather avoided mandatory military service in his native Germany by emigrating to the US attracted by the gold rush. After unsuccessful efforts at prospecting, he became a vendor and operated a brothel which became the initial source of the trump family wealth.

Between 1905-1907, with a 6 month pregnant wife bearing Fred (trump's father) the grandfather sought to repatriate to his homeland and was forbidden because of his avoidance of the required military service that he evaded by emigrating to America and over a 147 year span not one member of trump's family (great or grandparent, parent, uncle, son, cousin, nephew or grandkids) ever served in any military.

In my opinion, I believe this part of the family history is what has influenced trump's adherence to White supremacy where he enjoys popularity among all such groups in the country as well as his attraction and strong affinity to become a Hitler like leader in the US which is why trump's desperate pursuit of the presidency in 2024 must be defeated. With his fascist inclinations trump's objective is not just to avoid criminal accountability by winning back the White House in 2024 but to abruptly corrupt, disrupt and destroy democracy as we know it and any citizen who votes for this racist criminal again can never be referred to as a patriot of this country.

In the 70s, he was sued for refusing to rent to Blacks, he referred to African nations as shithole countries, his administration promoted anti-civil rights policies, he said all Haitians have Aids, he advocated for the death penalty for 5 innocent men in the 80s and he attacked Kaepernick for protesting racial injustice acts. There are many more examples that substantiates my claim that trump is a racist. With the certainty of an ongoing pattern of his criminal conduct established in nearly 100 indictments in state, civil and federal courts, we can count on trump resorting to frivolous litigious court filings as a defense.

He has no legitimate legal defense and he truly believes that if he can win the 2024 presidential election it will shield him from accountability. Any sound individual regardless of prior affinities for trump cannot in good conscious vote for him unless you happen to be empaneled as a juror in one of his cases and your vote is to convict.

As of February 2023 one in four members of the Republican caucus are proponents of the Qanon theories and at least 70% of them humiliatingly believe the 2020 presidential election was stolen. Qanon is a weak movement masquerading as a strong one whose followers await on-line clues from an unseen and unknown source. Its morally impoverished adherents try to decode or decipher these clues (many with racist or separatist overtones) in order to determine its message. The Qanon concept closely resembles the opening dialog from the fictionalized 1960s TV series Mission Impossible. The difference is in the TV series the message was concise whereas Qanon's is vague and its translation is subjected to misinterpretation by its adherents.

For the purpose of indoctrination, Qanon has at least a dozen designated personalities who supposedly have the capacity to discern the Qanon messages and each of these personalities has hundreds of thousands of followers who are being used as pawns in a political game. This is what trump and his new breed of Republicans subscribe to while falsely declaring we're living in a post racial society as they subtly pursue White dominance. As a movement the small victories they've experienced has impacted, attracted, reverberated, and influenced potential adherents across the nation.

Even the corroded, compromised and corrupt congressional Republicans ascribes to the great replacement theory, established in 2012 by Frenchman Renaud Camus, which asserts that there is a plot which has White culture disappearing due to immigration from non-White countries that will eventually lead to the persecution of Whites in this country. Such beliefs have motivated the Christchurch shooting in New Zealand and the El Paso Texas shooting. Qanon's theory itself is a pile of fascist garbage that has a historical trajectory identical to e formation of the American Nazi Party and has even found a home among a substantial chunk of the dangerous and extremist Republican electorate in the US Congress.

One can disagree with my characterizations but where am I wrong. As an incurable optimist let me articulate one of the reasons why congressional republicans are captivated by trump and why his Maga cultic supporters have yet to abandon him. The former group with an unquenchable thirst for power believes trump empowers them politically and the latter group which rejects progressive social change seeks dominance over everyone outside of their cult will undoubtedly go to war against this country if commanded to do so by trump. A review of what happened on J6th should sufficiently substantiate this assertion.

A number of billionaire media owners such as Elon Musk and R. Murdoch to name a few are non-journalistic and adverse to accurate reporting of news its viewers need to hear. Instead of monitoring for accuracy the false information received from or about trump they contrive biased corporate narratives and embeds it into their broadcasts. It accounts for much of the distorted and divisive information which like a stimulant influences its viewers about what's happening on the political landscape. They regularly transcribe propaganda and present it as news effectively misleading and further polarizing viewers relying on these media sources for their information and who believe they're being enlightened by those distorted reports. Sometimes the misleading reports when fact checked and proven false gets retracted but many viewers who've ingested to erroneous information are not around for the retraction. The repetitive scripted broadcasts from their prolific disinformation chambers are produced mainly for-profit motives and at times to provide favorable coverage for their endorsed candidates in elections.

The aforementioned news agencies in addition to host of obscure crop-ups are all willing to brazenly and cynically elevate falsehoods to feed to viewers via their, disreputable hosts masquerading as journalists, instead of offering credible information in service of the public interest. So I urge all of my readers, in search of the truth, to be critical thinkers and to find other supporting or corroborating sources for the information you may find on Twitter and Fox. The Fox network anchors knowingly and intentionally distort the truth through omission and exaggeration then disguise it as news. They seemingly have a loathing contempt for its viewers, most are avowed conspiracy theorists who regularly promote the great replacement theory on prime-time TV which undoubtedly perpetuates the polarizing dissension and division found among its viewers and nonviewers.

The host are prolific in utilizing their broadcast to manipulate the minds of its viewers by making the innocent look guilty and the guilty look innocent. Fox has become a disinformation echo chamber where broadcasts are now regularly replete with misstatements and misrepresentations which should trigger questions about their validity as a legitimate news organization. Laura Ingraham, Sean Hannity and Sucker Carlson are complicit trump buffoons who've effectively become a propaganda arm of the Republican party and Russia.

On their broadcasts they openly advocate on trump's behalf and that idiot Laura Ingraham went so far as threatening to primary any republican who supported a senate proposed immigration bill because she thinks the absence of such a bill would strengthen trump's argument on the issue as he campaigns for 2024. Because of their viewers love and idolization of trump the Fox network discriminatory suppression of accurately reporting trump's disqualifying unstable behavior accounts for why trump is leading all Republican contenders for the party's 2024 nomination. Fox anchors, dissatisfied with Fox White House reporter Jacqui Heinrich who once fact checked a tweet by trump, when top election officials insured that there was no evidence of any voting systems being compromised in 2020 and they tried to get her fired for reporting the truth.

Other than trump the FOX network and a number of obscure news companies has contributed to misleading its viewers by knowingly spewing propaganda and lies which attracts more far right Republicans guest to these networks. They know the lies they spew will not be fact checked by the hosts of those networks because they too explicitly question the integrity of the entire US justice system with inflammatory characterizations stripped of proper context. These self-proclaimed news agencies endorses an alarming series of conspiracy theories related to J6th, the Covid-19 vaccine and the validity of the 2020 election. With exception of Jessica Tarlov, the anchors and the CEO of Fox are existential threats to our democracy who all knew trump's insistence the election was stolen was false yet repeatedly contradicted their true views and regurgitated the stolen election nonsense to appease trump.

Publicly released text exchanges between Fox anchors and it's CEO stipulates they knew the election wasn't stolen but agreed to air the lie anyway so they wouldn't lose viewers. Their lies and pretending helped fuel the dissension which led to an insurrection on J6th. Fox was more concerned about its stock prices going down than the truth so they wittingly engaged in a disinformation campaign for money and ratings by deliberately embedding false stories in their daily broadcasts despite consequently subjecting itself civil liability.

They should no longer be shielded from liability and I believe punitive FCC regulations are needed for the deliberate widespread deception by the media. Fox secretly conveyed Biden's advertising to the trump campaign in 2020 and is embroiled in a multi-billion-dollar lawsuit for its horrendous lies against Dominion Voting machines and another voting technology company Smartmatic recently filled a 2.7-billion-dollar suit against Fox. One of Fox's main host Sucker Carlson, more than two years after January 6th was given by the house speaker 41 hours of unseen video of the Capital on January 6th. Carlson cherry picked through the footage and released selective portions which preceded the violence to substantiate his erroneous version of what actually occurred on J 6th. Carlson's deceptive efforts here seemingly suggest his viewers disbelieve what they have already seen and know about J6th and to believe his lies instead.

Chapter 5

The most shameful act by the Republicans, besides the fact that they're embracing stances which alienates huge swaths of voters who don't support them, is that in 2016 they trusted an unethical, lying, immoral and criminal political arsonist named trump to become the leader of the party and their complicity was not compelled it was voluntarily extended. With no fidelity to the Constitution, no ability to lead the nation and unmatched levels of corruption exceeded only by his defiant sense of entitlement, trump's corrosive toxicity has prompted an erosion of the legitimacy of the entire Republican party.

If one intends to be in the presence of trump, it would be advisable to wear boots and carry a shovel for extraction because the oral excrement that emanates from him can be deep and smothering with the capacity to capture and convert the naive. The majority of trump's criticisms, complaints and accusations of his opponents are no more than projections that when inversely applied are accurate representations of himself. Although I've fortunately never been, nor desire to be in his presence, my inferences and observations are made from a distant vantage point (media sources) which shields me from contamination of his toxic influences. With his profound ability to create and exploit tension and the exposure of his many improprieties one would be hard pressed to sincerely ascribe to trump any of the virtuous quality traits all former presidents to some degree have exhibited.

Among all former and even the current president, trump exclusively possesses high corrosive and subversive levels of hypocrisy that appeal to his cultic Maga base and he's threatened to diminish or obliterate our Democracy, displaying our fragility to the watching world. Here's a long list of qualities he lacks: he has no class, no charm, no credibility, no compassion, no sensitivity, no wisdom, no honor and no grace. All former presidents were generously blessed with a number of these attributes along with a commitment to defend our democracy which is in stark contrast to and highlights the embarrassing limitations of trump as president.

He's famous for his crude witless insults and bullying tactics except when he's among bullies like Putin or Kim he's reduced to a sniveling sidekick. The stench of his malfeasance cannot be hidden and he loves to kick the vulnerable and the voiceless especially when they're down which violates the unspoken rule of basic human decency. One does not need a particularly keen eye for detail to spot trump's glaring faults and flaws which are numerous and hard to miss. He turns being artless into an art form, he makes Nixon look trustworthy, he makes Bush look smart, he's a Picasso of pettiness, the architect of appalling and a Shakespeare of shit. There have always been stupid people in the world and plenty of nasty people too but only with trump has stupidity been so nasty and nastiness so stupid.

Since congressional republicans are failing in their constitutional duties it is our obligation to dilute trump's

Maga influence that weighs like disgusting albatross around the neck of the nation. Congress has refused, despite inculpatory evidence, to hold him accountable for any of his miserably failed pre or post election promises even as he constantly exhibited elements of contempt and contention for congressional oversight. The following is a list of corroborative examples:

He didn't lower our taxes but he did lower the taxes for the wealthy.

He never proposed a plan for infrastructure after bragging of his supposed proficiency in the construction business.

He didn't replace Obama care with something g better and in four years never presented any proposal to do so.

He failed to decrease the deficit instead he raised it 25% in just four years which is a historical record for any president.

He totally failed in the opioid crisis.

He didn't make Covid-19 disappear.

He didn't make Mexico pay for the wall of which only 20% of the 400 miles completed was new. The other 80% was existing barriers that was reinforced.

He didn't put America first and personally made 19 million dollars in foreign transactions while in office.

Not only did he fail to drain the swamp he saturated it with more slime.

He revived the coal industry instead of seeking alternative sources of energy.

One thing he achieved which was never a campaign promise is he validated hate throughout the country and openly embraced White supremacy.

He criticized Obama for playing too much golf and vowed to avoid playing as much. During his one term, cumulatively an entire year was wasted as he made over 250 trips to his golf properties at a cost of over $130 million which included secret service detail and their accommodations at his property.

These trips were strategic efforts to prop up his stagnant golf courses by generating taxpayer funds for his underperforming courses. The following is a list of his bankruptcies and other business failures which overshadows the aforementioned list of his broken promises:

In 1991 trump Taj Mahal casino in Atlantic City filed for bankruptcy.

The trump Plaza, The trump Castle and the Plaza Hotel all owned by trump filed for bankruptcy in 1992.

Trump Hotels & Casino Resorts(THCR) founded by trump in 1995 filed for bankruptcy in 2004.

Trump Entertainment Resorts Inc the new name given to THCR in 2004 filed for bankruptcy in 2009.

The following businesses had a licensing agreement with trump and they all failed:

The trump shuttle formerly owned by Eastern Airlines was taken over by trump in 1989, defaulted on its loan in 1990 and was bankrupt by 1992.

Trump University founded in 2005 went out of business by 2011 because of unethical business practices.

Drinks America Co under license from trump produced trump vodka in 2005 was discontinued in 2011.

A financial services company Trump Mortgage LLC founded in 2006 ceased in 2007.

A travel site Go trump.com also founded in 2006 ceased operations in 2007.

Trump Steaks founded in 2007 by trump discontinued sales two months after its launch.

The USFL NJ Generals was brought by trump in 1983 who hoped it would translate into ownership of an NFL franchise. The USFL folded before the start of the 1986 season and trump never came close to owning an NFL team.

Don't be surprised that along with trump and far too many members of Congress, came a resurgence of White supremacy throughout the nation because he is an authentic genuine racist himself who has exposed a number of like-minded congressmen and as the saying goes birds of a feather flock together. Right-wing media strategically bombards their broadcasts with trump's false concepts and disinformation about J6th and constantly promotes his anti-democratic agenda. One must not forget that as president he employed a cast of alleged and convicted criminals in high level positions:

Peter Navarro, convicted and sentenced

Trump lawyers Powell and Cheseboro convicted

Allen Weisselberg, convicted and sentenced

Jared Ivanka Kushner, received over $4billion combined in shady business dealings

Paul Manafort, convicted, imprisoned then pardoned

Rick Gates, convicted and sentenced to prison

Roger Stone convicted, sentenced then pardoned

Mike Flynn, convicted sentenced then pardoned

George Papadopoulos, convicted and sentenced to prison

Steve Bannon, charges pending for fraud and money laundering and was convicted for defying a subpoena.

And all of these criminals meet trump's standard qualifications for service if he's reelected in addition to many other immoral characters he has in queue. Also one must be reminded that over the years trump has had at 27 allegations of sexual assault against him.

There are overwhelming amounts of credible evidence that trump inspired the J6th riot which was predicated on his defiant espousal of a stolen 2020 election conspiracy theory. Additionally his selling of fear and anxiety around the issues of crime and immigration along with his silence and indifference about guns and school shootings reflects the inherent immutable qualities of his deceptive lying and his discontent for minorities which is propelling our democracy to the brink of destruction. With the co-opted aid of divisive, dysfunctional and spineless Republican congressmen, trump's contorted interpretation of the constitution has created a polarizing dissension that's spreading like wildfire across the country while constantly fomenting hostility towards the press which incrementally increases the polarity in the nation and exacerbates the threat of civil war. His increasing attacks on the judicial system, witnesses, former aides, state officials and anyone attempting to hold him accountable subjects them all to regular threats from the Maga crowd.

The former TV show host trump who claims to be well schooled is really not well educated, constantly espouses fascist rhetoric and is a grifter with an unquenchable thirst for money and power. He is desperately seeking office in 2024, compelled to do so primarily to escape criminal accountability and to further enrich his family and himself. His unwavering Maga supporters subscribe to his incessant attacks on the judicial system and our elections and he has easily undermined the once respectable but now debilitated and radicalized congressional Republicans because of their perceived fears of being voted out of office without trump's support.

Their trafficking in extremism and delusional fabricated claims reveals they want nothing other than total power and on January 6th they were prepared to seize it when trump utilized a proverbial gasoline and matches routine. His biggest mistake was after pouring the gas he entrusted his vice president to light the match and Pence's refusal to do so preserved our Democracy, at least for now. Pence's action on J6th combined with trump's loss of the 2020 election and the rejection of a tainted election claim by over 60 courts all contributed to the prevention of the fall of our democracy. In a desperate quest for power the congressional Republicans have devolved into legislative terrorists who appear primed to give trump the party's nomination for 2024 despite his blatant criminal activity and if he is elected again don't count on him entrusting anyone else to light the metaphorical match, he'll do it himself.

The thing that should scare all Americans if trump is elected in 2024 is that it will represent the birth of fascism in America with swift retribution or violence against his opponents, continual use of war rhetoric domestically as a tool to subvert democratic norms and denigrating the judiciary until he finds a way to remake and control it. The threat exists simply because too many of his supporters have hidden behind or dismissed trump's ideas, as serious but not literal or literal but not serious. The fact is trump is laying the groundwork through his campaign for vindication and retribution for the false stolen election and should be taken literally and seriously about his expressed plans to retaliate against opponents.

One would be hard-pressed to find any other citizen in the country regardless of qualifications who'd remain in contention for the highest office in the nation despite a Civil sexual assault conviction and 91 pending criminal charges but in a desperate efforts to escape justice that's where trump finds himself. And with his authoritarian aspirations if reelected trump will try to control the media, the judiciary and oversight of the legislature just like Putin does in Russia. And rather than subject himself to judicial scrutiny for all of the crimes he committed he'd rather his ill-informed fanatical counter patriotism supporters interfere on his behalf as in Georgia where it was announced that the Republican led legislature proposed a law empowering itself with the ability to remove prosecutors and the Republican governor is waiting to sign it into law.

A criminal investigation of trump in Georgia concluded with grand jury referrals and trump's indictment is imminent. But Republican congressmen in DC, intent on promoting absurd disinformation and interference campaigns have undertook efforts to corrupt any investigations and has signaled concurrence with GA legislators as they seek the removal of the Georgia DA in an attempt to protect trump. This sort of manipulative maneuvering by a political party would be unthinkable a decade ago but the frayed sense of solidarity between the two political party's which prevents any reasonable debate among themselves consequently has led to the unrecognizable tapestry of the foundation of this country and to the visible tattered fabrics of our torn democracy.

Hopefully with all of trump's mounting legal troubles he'll be disqualified from seeking any public office by 2024. He is banking heavily on favorable rulings and interference from the courts he and McConnell helped pack with unqualified inexperienced judges who he believes are indebted to him. Former members of his administration, Kushner and Mnuchin to name a few, have financially benefitted after leaving demonstrating their positions were covers for their self-serving grift.

The fact that those two combined have received over 3 billion dollars substantiates my contention that trump's administration was predicated on foreign corruption and anyone voting for trump in 2024 is complicit in sabotaging American values and destabilizing the rule of law. The former senate majority leader McConnell (a lap dog for trump) deliberately stopped holding confirmation hearings for all judicial nominees during Obama's final two years and expedited hearings for trump nominees culminating in the packing of the courts with numerous unqualified judges. Republicans aided by McConnell citing an unfounded rule of the Senate stole a SCOTUS pick from Obama 8 months before his second term ended hypocritically accelerated a trump SCOTUS nominee 8 days before the end of his term. Consequently we have ultra-conservative SCOTUS members wholesaley purchased and heavily influenced by

Corporate America and billionaire donors. Donors who influence the corruption and impact the decisions of conservative justices in cases heard or rejected by the court in which those donors have vested interest in the outcome. Some recent cases where the Court's decision was influenced by outside forces were the overturning of Roe v Wade, rejecting student debt loan forgiveness and rolling back affirmative action. Without blatant targeted congressional republican interference the balance on the Court would rightfully be 5 to 4 favoring liberals.

For a one term president, trump has had the 2nd most appointment to the federal bench in presidential history. Potentially his 231 appointments (3 SCOTUS, 54 Circuit Court, 174 District Court)to the federal bench for lifetime appointments can adversely impact the nation as these judges are vital to the citizenry of the nation because its where all lawsuits involving the constitution or laws made by Congress are litigated. A number of trump nominees to the courts were deemed unqualified yet despite these determinations many made it through confirmation after meeting republican's criteria of being against voting rights and women's reproductive protections.

At the beginning of trump's administration he was thrilled at the number of judicial vacancies thanks to McConnell's illicit means to gain a majority on the SCOTUS which included denying hearings for Obama's nominees. Consequently trump received a gift of three SCOTUS seats to fill and since these appointments the court has seen an erosion of its legitimacy and has become unethical and overtaken by scandal. The SCOTUS bypasses its traditional process of determining what cases will appear before the court in order to adversely expedite its rollback of precedent benefitting the public and to satisfy the far right and corporations.

Not only is it reaching decisions that are questionable and unpopular it is susceptible to influence peddling due to expectations of its loyalty to trump and his Maga mobsters. The chief Justice of the court wife made at least 10 million dollars over four years as a recruiter for firms with business pending before the court. Justice Clarence Thomas has been involved in a massive decades long string of corruption where millionaires and billionaires paid for among other things at least 38 of Thomas's annual vacations, paid for his wedding reception, school tuition for a relative and purchased Thomas's mother home way over market value, paid 267K for a luxury motor coach RV, yacht voyages, at least 26 private jet flights plus an additional 8 helicopter flights. Justice Gorsuch and Justice Alito both have had questionable ethical transactions which can be perceived as influence peddling with donors who had material interests in cases before the court. These conservative justices have adopted an absence of understanding yet they make regular rulings on our rights and claim to have character, integrity and the highest level of ethics. Some have developed an appetite for an immersion in bribery, simultaneously influencing their decisions and subjecting the justice system to external and biased partisan influence.

Institutional policing exists on all judicial levels except for the Supreme Court and should immediately be adopted and applied in light of recent reports of a number of Justices being allegedly influenced by donors. This self policing insures that the judiciary maintains its own standards by holding members accountable for not standing up to the values professed by the judiciary and it applies appropriate discipline to members in violation of its rules. The appearance of being pro-corporate or the reality of impropriety among some Justices diminishes and undermines the Court's legitimacy and at best should be disqualifying for them or at least warrant recusal from cases with ethical questions and concerns. Recent exposure of the dealings of a few SCOTUS Justices reveals to their detriment that some use their prestigious position for their personal benefit rather than on behalf of the public or upholding the constitution which warrants immediate reform of the SCOTUS.

In order to accommodate a host of trump's judicial nominees McConnell conducted express hearings and even refused to honor an informal century's old Senate rule which prevented nominees from being confirmed without the vote of their home state senator. The 9th Circuit Court of Appeals have five new judges now because McConnell refused to hold a vote for an Obama nominee then swiftly held votes for four trump nominees without approval of their home state senator.

McConnell's objective was to appoint and confirm strict conservative judges in their 40s or 50s to these lifetime positions who would be amenable to roll back voting rights, civil rights, rights on contraceptives and abortion. They appear to be winning as they advance their hierarchal framework of power, dominance and aggression on a national scale. One cannot deny their strategy has been effective and efficient to that end primarily because of an uninformed electorate which needs to be transformed into a literate electorate that can make informed judgements about potential candidates.

This will afford voters the capacity to form their own conclusions and it eliminates a large segment of voter reliance on the Fox and other obscure propaganda networks where conclusions are handed to you. We can't allow trump to be elected to the distinguished office of president only to denigrate and disgrace it again because the failures in his first term won't be repeated. One example of a failure was his 2020 executive order Schedule F, which would have allowed him to make tens and potentially hundreds of thousands career officials become political appointees effectively stripping away job protections.

This would've allowed trump to fire civil servants who fail his loyalty test. Before Schedule F could be implemented trump ran out of time and Biden rescinded it when he took office. If given another term an aggressive purge of the Civil service will be trump's top priority. Also trump's closest competitor for the 2024 Republican nomination Ron DeSantis shares the Schedule F idea.

With the number of judges trump has nominated his hope now is that his pending civil and eventual criminal cases will land in one of their courtrooms and he receive a favorable ruling. For example: his documents case in Florida was assigned to a judicial appointee of his who disregarded ethical jurisprudence and made rulings in his favor that were eventually struck down in the Court of Appeals. If democracy survives or falls the Court's will be instrumental in the outcome. There is a taboo term in Congress called packing the Court which Republicans abhor and are adamantly opposed to but have been secretly engaged in. I find it very offensive that the thing they claim to now oppose is what they eagerly participated in during trump's term in office. This court is on a warpath to strip away rights of Americans. It has already watered down voting rights of the Civil Rights era, they've overturned Roe vs Wade and have stripped away the rights of defendants to challenge convictions on the basis of ineffective counsel and there is likely more to come.

The SCOTUS has rendered decisions, rewritten laws and redefined rights that'll adversely reverberate in our society for many years. It has made decisions that maintained the conservative causes of major donors and corporations whose broad policy and political interests were at stake. Another thing that should concern us about the SCOTUS and trump's appointment of unqualified judges to the federal bench is that they are strategically positioned to denigrate the rule of law and make dilatory decisions on his behalf. In 2024, the nation is witnessing the perilous delegitimization of both its federal and state judiciaries as well as the systematic dismantling of the rule of law by a single man, the former president of the United States. Never in the nation's history has anyone, engaged in their own defense civilly or criminally, brazenly leveled threatening attacks against judges and their family members, court staff and witnesses but were met only with passivity from the courts. This manipulative conman has fractured the judiciary and successfully enlisted the SCOTUS in his efforts to delay every one of his pending criminal trials. With the judiciary and HOR republicans loyally aligned with him we can expect no resistance from either of these sources if trump wins in 2024 and tries to impose an authoritarian model of government. Now let us survey congress.

The following is the service obligation for all congressmen:

Through legislative debate and compromise the US Congress makes laws that influence our lives. It holds hearings to inform the legislative process, conducts investigations to oversee the executive branch and serves as the voice of the people and the states in the federal government. The lack of etiquette and decorum has too many mealy-mouthed MAGA members of Congress failing in the latter part of this obligation as they attempt to subvert the democratic process while trafficking in and seeking to gain power through disinformation campaigns which has transformed many congressmen from lawmakers into potential lawbreakers. Through right wing populism, extremism and the influential sway over their voter base, they're defending a deceptive, destructive, misguided, idiotic wanna be dictator named trump (who's the conduit for their rage) through two impeachments and are intent on rescuing him from accountability for his numerous criminal charges.

As trump's unpopularity increases along with his legal issues, I don't anticipate this extreme MAGA wing of the GOP driven, dominated, and intimidated by this fascist leaning trump, will prevail in rescuing him from his impending legal troubles. They've abandoned the principles of the GOP and their legitimacy has been nullified due to unyielding efforts to shield trump from accountability for his conduct and his unparalleled level of idiocy which directly puts them in violation of their oath's to uphold the constitution. HOR republicans continuing support for trump whose coded language has fanned the flames of White supremacy in the nation illustrates their exceptionally high threshold for humiliation and exhibits their volitional self-abasement.

Their acceptance of his 91 indictments, two impeachments and J6th should be sufficient prerequisites for disqualification from Congress. Republican congressmen have abandoned their legitimacy and have been discredited as legislators. They frequently conduct sham hearings masquerading as legislation and have repeatedly mischaracterized testimony of witnesses appearing before its committee when that testimony dispels their erroneous theories of Biden's involvement in his son's business dealings. There's been an abandonment of obligation and duty among HOR republicans whose pattern and practice is to cherry pick through noncredible information and promote it as evidence disregarding the fact of it being previously debunked. With a laser like focus they're preoccupied with investigating Hunter Biden with the hope of ensnaring Joe Biden but they fail to take an interest in or give any warranted scrutiny to the (real crime family) trump's.

At times, to fool or impress their supporters and appear to be engaged in true legislation they may propose some milk toast partisan bill refusing to acknowledge that any partisan bill they generate will be decimated by two democratically controlled bodies in the Senate and White House. They avoid any meaningful bipartisan cooperation on legislation that would impact the American people such as securing funds to increase border security while they boisterously complain and blame Biden for the decades old border failure. Not all congressional republicans are impoverished both morally and ethically but the majority are Maga extremists who through their silence, embraces the extremists ideology, rendering them complicit with the trump mobster agenda. The tax cuts they hand out to their wealthy donors emanates from a quid pro and results in the economy slowing while the deficit grows. Their remedy to offset this imbalance always is to suggest reforms to entitlements like Social Security/Medicare and to mischaracterize the expense incurred by illegal immigration. This clearly illustrates their priorities are never concern for seniors or those with disabilities but always for the wealthy. It's ironic that they come to us to get elected only to sell us out to the highest bidders. One recurring theme in this book has been that self-serving Maga mobsters in Congress care only about trump and power while pretending to love law and order.

In early 2023 the Republican chairman of a congressional committee threatened Direct TV executives who pulled from its own network, an obscure News agency sponsoring propaganda and promoting conspiracy theories, which the committee chairman wanted restored to the Direct TV broadcast. Most republican members of the 118th Congress accept trump's insistence the 2020 election was stolen and they're supporting and concocting election conspiracy theories as if trump actually won. This is as ridiculous as going to the lottery claim center claiming to have won the grand prize and you're not in possession of a ticket for validation. This appalling trump support by Republican congressmen clearly reflects their immoral agenda and their failure as a party, on every parameter and barometer one could use to measure. Their failure has contributed to trump's capture of their party which expeditiously has placed the country on a path of descent fueled by a polarizing dissension and birthed by an abject failure to uphold their official obligatory duties.

55

Chapter 6

HOR Republicans have descended to the depths of dissension that's rapidly spreading among their voter base and they've intensely debased themselves by their futile cowardly submission to trump. They're enveloped in trump's subversive inclinations and being shrouded in their self-induced stupor have yielded total control of the party to trump resulting in division and dysfunction among colleagues along with a gradual loss of many supporters. They've massively deluded themselves into thinking they can best lead the country and have become proficient in the tactic of aggressive defensiveness which projects democrats and left leaning groups as scapegoats for the polarizing and often criminal conduct of right-wingers and trump. Maga indoctrinated adherents are seemingly experiencing trump induced cognitive dissonance and persistently subscribe to theories that don't even make sense to themselves.

HOR members such as Gaetz, Boebert, Jordan, Green and B. Donalds are regrettably nothing but self-aggrandizing sociopaths whose embarrassing allegiance to trump is solely what keeps him relevant and situated to upend democracy in 2024. As leaders of the 118th Congress their incompetence and insanity propels them to promoting an agenda filled with unhinged fractious rhetoric and they are interested in politics only as performance art as well as a distraction to shield trump. If they we're just a fringe minority within the party they would not be a threat but 97% of HOR republicans directly or by silent complicity are Maga adherents. Some of these leaders are on a tantrum of anger, criticism and accusations against Biden who did nothing but win an election which the diaper wearing orange bunker man claims to have won.

Their failure in the aftermath of J6th to protect the integrity of our institutions was on full display as they were dismissive of the disorder and oblivious to the violent tensions inflamed by trump when he summoned and unleashed a violent mob, culminating into an insurrection on that day. They've chosen to ignore the transparent aspirations of trump who is spearheading the demise of the enduring values of our democracy, who persistently defrauds people, doesn't pay his bills, who lies like breathing and was responsible for them running in fear or cowering under desks from a mob of invaders on J6th. And they're predisposed to vote for him again despite him being separately convicted civilly of sexual assault and fraud resulting in over $500 million in fines with 91 criminal charges pending. He is exhibiting signs of rapid cognitive decline at his cultic campaign rallies and he constantly proposes vengeance and retribution against his political foes.

An unbiased review of his time in office will undoubtedly illustrate and verify conclusively an elaborate deficiency of qualifications or capacity to be president. Yet despite his incendiary rhetoric and lack of any substantive policies he remains the front-runner for the party's nomination. One would have to be in the throws of a toxic delusion to ignore the list of his disqualifying characteristics: he's never been emotionally, ethically, intellectually or psychologically fit to be president. Some of his most appalling behavior resulted in two impeachments, he attempted to steal an election, he has a penchant to cozy up with domestic and international crooks, his deceptiveness and his horrible mishandling of Covid-19 which led to more than 1 million deaths (400K in 11 months under trump) all has been dismissed and ignored by Republicans who've voluntarily pledged blind loyalty to him.

Ever since trump captured control of the GOP the self-emasculating descent of the republicans now sullying the halls of the Capitol has resulted in the abdication of duties and responsibilities and triggered a radical departure from political, traditional and legal norms thereby placing them on a calamitous path. Congressional actions they've initiated for over a year appallingly appear to be attributive in furtherance of their plans to restore trump to office which we must ensure is a losing proposition. A committee to evaluate the DOJ created by these right-wing conspiracy theorists and ironically named "Weaponization of the Government" withholds from democrat members, subject matter of hearings it conducts in an effort to thwart opposition research. It is investigating whether Biden has weaponized the DOJ yet refuses to delve into matters related to investigating trump, or parents threatening school board members or the fire bombing of right to life offices. DOJ is investigating the above mentioned matters but apparently not to this House committee's satisfaction.

This diluted, polluted, legislatively impotent committee is being used as a place to settle scores for trump, showcase conspiracy theories and advance an extremists agenda which undermines Americans faith in our democracy.This committee is tainted and stained by the presence of radical trump supporting sycophantic members who realize that a true investigation of the weaponization of the DOJ (which repeatedly occurred under trump) would be perilous for the desperate political aspirations of trump recapturing the White House. The following are instances of trump's incontrovertible weaponizaton of the DOJ:

Ordering the IRS conduct an intense audit on former FBI officials who had investigated his connections to Russia while preventing the agency from auditing himself ordering that a, provisionally mandated by the constitution, request for his tax record be denied to congress.

He outrageously and improperly used the SDNY offices to punish his enemies and protect his friends.

He disgracefully turned DOJ into his personal law firm by installing people who would do his bidding.

He had his second AG Barr to remove any US Attorneys who trump perceived as a threat to his agenda.

He pardoned Steve Bannon, who was being investigated for his involvement with the We Build the Wall campaign, with an imminent indictment pending.

He had Barr get Michael Cohen's home confinement rescinded and returned to prison because Cohen proceeded with a book deal.

He asked his AG to go light on sentencing Roger Stone against the advice of prosecutors which is unheard of since Watergate.

He made the Michael Flynn case go away against the interests of the prosecutor.

He had his AG investigate the investigators of trump's Russian collusion.

He instructed the DOJ without any evidence to say that the 2020 election was corrupt and to leave the rest to him and his republican congressmen while he was preparing to replace acting Attorney General Rosen with lap dog Jeffrey Clark, who had letters falsely citing voter fraud, prepared to be sent to state legislatures where trump had lost the vote.

There's more examples of this manic menace efforts to politicize and weaponize the DOJ and the following list clearly illustrates a pattern of other abuses of power by trump such as:

Abuse of the pardon powers
The firing of whistle blowers and truth tellers
Enriching his family and himself
Requiring loyalty of staff and aides
Subverting an election
Inciting an insurrection
Preventing cooperation of staff with congressional investigations
Withholding reinforcements for officers being violently attacked on J6th

All which warrant congressional scrutiny yet no committee, other than the special committee formed for J6th, has expressed an interest to investigate anything related to the malignant narcissistic former president. Neither the trump dominated news agencies nor his congressional cohorts accurately ascribe to him sentiments which reflects his blatant criminality and they avoid exposing his direct implicit oral assaults articulated against his opposition because this will expose him to the broader public. Instead they shamefully focus on frivolous cultural war issues that trump regularly promotes at his clown shows which he calls rallies.

This perfectly represents how far the party has fallen and is indicative of the threat they've become as they embrace wholeheartedly the MAGA agenda which was soundly rejected by 2022 midterm voters and will likely be rejected in 2024 when faced with deciding whether to vote for a man with 81 years behind him or a man with 92 indictments in front of him. Instead of crafting a credible plan to tackle inflation that is hurting all Americans, Republicans have a laser like focus on investigating Hunter Biden and as proxies for Putin are trying to cut off aid to Ukraine in its war against Russia.

In 2024, we must insulate our democracy from the dangerous threat clearly represented by a misguided, partisan, loyalist group of Maga mobsters who follow a con man whose extremism has been exposed as contaminating. Metaphorically, the democracy diminishing train came to town at the invitation of trump in 2017 and right-wing extremists in Congress eagerly hopped aboard and when made aware of its destination they lack any courage to get off deciding instead to enjoy the ride. Leadership in this new congress consists of a strange cast of extremists who regularly parrot Putin propaganda and sides with the Russian invasion of Ukraine. HOR Republicans, now synonymous with Russians, have abandoned their most historic and consistent trait of being antagonistically opposed to the

Soviet Union. It's glaringly apparent that the HOR republicans have become the heartbeat of pro-Putin elements in American politics due to its adherence to Maga's persuasions. The following HOR members are just a few of the many within the party characterized or categorized as being fully aligned with the pro-Putin agenda now prevalent in the party prompting the immense degradation of America's world standing and power:

1) Jim (Gym) Jordan: the ignorant, fast talking but slow thinking former assistant wrestling coach at Ohio State university (1987-1995) whose depth of depravity was on full display as he aided and abetted sexual abuse by a OSU team doctor when he ignored the reported abuse by team members. Gym refused to act on the truthful complaints of those students yet he quickly and boisterously defends the stolen election lies of trump. He even feigned uncertainty when questioned about whether he was in consultation with trump as January 6th was being planned. We know that Gym was involved in trump's planning for J6th and was on the phone with trump at 8 a.m. on the morning of J6th and likely had several other contacts throughout that day.

Yet he ignored and defied a subpoena on that matter and is hypocritically advocating for Hunter Biden to be held in contempt for defying a subpoena. Mesmerizingly stupid, this clown Gym Jordan went to law school but never passed a bar exam in any state and with over 16 years in Congress has never been the lead sponsor of a single bill that became law ranking him among the least effective house members ever. But as Judiciary Committee chairman he's been steadfastly running interference for trump and has repeatedly attempted to manipulate the purpose of the committee in order to attack democrats and to vociferously support and protect trump. There's no interest in crafting any legislation that would benefit the American people and for the entirety of this legislative session they've been preoccupied with illegitimate investigations. Gym foolishly became an active obstructionist when he was in contention with the NYDA over its investigation of trump and in his own arrogance and or ignorance he unethically requested, with the hope of producing bombshell revelations, that the NYDA appear before his committee which amounts to federal interference in a state investigation.

The committee chaired by obstructionist, dysfunctional and incompetent Jordan functions as if it were a law firm for trump and is oxymoronically named the Weaponization of Government Committee which rightfully should called the Committee to Obstruct Justice. It is purposely focused on non-existent weaponization claims against Biden while ignoring blatant violations of trump's administration. Jordan demonstrates daily a lack of critical thinking skills and has his committee blindly fishing in a toilet tank while an adjacent pond full of fish remains untapped.

2) Marjorie(the socks stay on) Greene whose depth of intellect is very shallow and who lacks any modicum of competence or decency is a radical, repugnant reactionary racist who was kicked off committees only one month into her 1st term for assertions reflective of an acknowledgement of her lunacy. She has aligned herself with Maga and White supremacy while disrespecting, denigrating and disparaging the Black community, Jews and immigrants. She's promoting

Jewish space laser theories, regurgitating Qanon theories, is a satanic worshipper, believes no plane crashed into the Pentagon on 9/11, the Las Vegas music festival was not the work of a lone gunman, the Clinton's murdered JFK Jr. and she harassed Parkland shooting survivors. In January 2023 she's returned to committee assignments and has become influential among the MAGA wing of the party who think the J6th insurrectionist are patriots, that January 6th was their 1776 and she endorses the execution of her democrat colleagues.

Greene is abject trash and an underwhelmingly talented fruitcake who criticized Biden for the number of US deaths caused by fentanyl then with her unmatched level of lunacy and idiotcracy on full display she cites as supportive evidence, data reflecting that seizures of fentanyl more than doubled under Biden as opposed to trump. Statements like this encapsulates what a despicable intellectually incapacitated ignorant dunce she is and how unqualified she is to represent any district in the HOR. Especially in light of her September 2023 proposed amendment to reduce the salary of Defense Secretary to $1 annually which would've been an appropriate proposal if applied to all of the MAGA obstructionist in Congress like herself rather than the Defense Secretary. She criticized Dr. Fauci as a nazi during the covid crisis but praises the nazi rhetoric of trump and she embarrassingly revealed herself when she was captured on camera supposedly mimicking a monkey so accurately that it triggered the question of whether in reality she is a member of the primate family. I may be wrong but one look at her feet persuaded me that she may be a primate. The absurdity of her public outbursts has gained her several monikers such as "Miserable Marge," "Qanon Karen," "Traitor Greene" and my favorite "The Socks Stay On."

3) Matt (pimpin the young girls) Gaetz: after being pulled over for speeding, was arrested in 2008 for DUI where he failed two eye tests then refused further field sobriety tests. Because his father was then a state senator Gaetz license wasn't suspended for a year as mandated by Florida law for refusing a breath test nor was his refusal used against him in his criminal proceedings. The charges were eventually dropped after the forced resignation of the arresting officer and the miraculous emergence of a anonymous civilian witness, who knew Gaetz, said they observed no indication of impairment by Gaetz. This person's testimony is all that contradicted the arresting officer's conclusion that there was probable cause to arrest Gaetz for DUI. He more recently was allegedly engaged in sex trafficking with underaged girls along with an associate who has since been convicted and mysteriously Gaetz, possibly because of family connections, was never charged. He participated in January 6th planning and sought a broad preemptive pardon before trump left office. Note that there's a rational, logical and moral distinction that one does not seek or accept a pardon without the consciousness of guilt.

4) Louis Gohmert: says January 6th perpetrators are political prisoners and drafted legislation to prevent their imprisonment and he advocated for having the ability to lie to the FBI and Congress.

5) Paul (my own siblings disown me) Gosar: who's so detached from reality that his six siblings have appeared in reelection campaign ads for his opponent and have strongly advised against voting for their brother who embraces bigoted, far-right and conspiratorial views.

6) Elise (the rotten beast) Stefanik a member since 2014 whose 2018 reelection was based on issues that matter to the public such as border security, inflation and government spending. This witting or unwitting useful idiot in 2024 as a leader in her party pledged to block any Senate bill increasing funding for border security solely to prevent Biden from being credited with fixing an issue republicans intend to run on in 2024. Her position was adopted to appease trump and to further ingratiate herself to trump as she aspires to be his running mate. The sellout Republican controlled HOR has failed to put forth a single bill to address any of the issues they claim to care about which reveals they can proficiently talk the talk but are totally inept in walking the walk. She was an avid trump defender in the first impeachment trial, voted against certifying the election after J6th and is a captive of trump who regularly parrots his radical ideas while pretending to believe in moderation in order to fool her voters in NY. She's become a trump loyalist who leads the charge in her party's baseless criticism of Biden's alleged responsibility for inflation despite inflation being a global issue and how comparably the US is managing better than any of the other developed countries.

As for government spending her party opposes Biden's social spending proposals like student debt relief, aid to Ukraine's fight against Russia but affirms aid to Israel's genocide in Palestine and never questioned trump who historically has been unmatched by any other president in terms of reckless spending. Her arrogance and belligerence, closely mirrors trump's. She is amoral, indecent, utterly reprehensible and is the reason for the resignation of two university president's at (Harvard and the University of Penn) after public forum questioning. The rotten character on display during the exchanges culminating in those resignations was not from the respondents but rather from the questioner Stefanik. She is the embodiment of this trend among Republicans who'll do anything that trump wants and have succumbed to the taste of power like a narcotic and will do anything for it such as shamefully referring to the violent criminally convicted J6th defendants as hostages. She's publicly provided aid, comfort and support to the Capitol rioters and promotes the false claim of Biden's weaponization of the Government while advocating for a criminal to be elected president. Her outrageous and dangerous position or opinion about trump reveals the comfort she has found in rejecting reality and disregarding the constitution as exhibited in her continuing unashamed trump support.

We should absolutely have no tolerance for her smug hypocrisy which accuses the entire democratic party of being antisemitic while being an apologist for a man who spits the venomous language of Hitler. Her avid adherence to the replacement theory which is foundational to the ideology of White nationalism and nazism unquestionably clear. There are citizens who're angry with the federal government and many justifiably so who need to be careful to not let their anger get them to fall for trump's and his sycophants like Stefanik lies that there's something better than the system we have. For our democracy to survive the ardent critics on Capitol Hill lies must be confronted directly, forcefully and relentlessly. As she pathetically operates in the cesspool of outrage without resolution Stefanik regularly campaigns on border issues yet resists bipartisan border remedies while spewing her lies that incite fear, create crisis and promotes a repugnant candidate for president in 2024. She feigns concern for border security with constant claims of house republicans being the last line of defense while simultaneously rejecting as instructed by trump a 14 billion-dollar Senate bill increasing funds to support border security because if this issue were resolved now trump would have less to attack, vilify and blame Biden for in his desperate campaign for 2024. Stefanik is a disgraceful proponent of lies intended to inflate public opinion of her party and she proudly defends Hitler's language being parroted by trump who aspires to replicate some of Hitler's actions if elected again. She engages in destructive misguided rhetoric when referring to the convicted J6th domestic terrorists as "hostages."

On trump's behalf and likely at his direction she made a judicial complaint in Nov. 2023 against the judge overseeing trump's NY civil fraud case and shortly afterwards she filed a judicial complaint against DC judge Howell for simply receiving an award from a renowned, prominent and bipartisan organization. She is a leader in the most ineffective Congress in recent history wasting a year preemptively conducting baseless investigations hoping to ensnare Biden into an impeachment which is nothing but a surreptitious effort to position her boss for victory in 2024. To view the

Republican caucus border policy metaphorically would resemble an out of control blaze rapidly approaching a residence with caucus members on the scene equipped with all the essentials to prevent the flames from engulfing the structure but they're awaiting the arsonist, who was complicit in starting the blaze for instructions on how to fight the flames. Stefanik stands at the forefront of helping trump evade accountability and she is a shameless fraud metamorphizing into something more evil, trump's potential VP running mate. In the face of the threat they represent we must be encouraged and remain vigilant as we face the procedural and political hurdles ahead. Our challenge to remove them may appear insurmountable because they're deeply entrenched in high levels of government but we who put them in office never relinquished our power to remove them. VOTE!

These six far-right HOR members along with numerous others like Byron Donald and Rick Perry are sick elements of a party, bereft of any decency, which aggressively instigate dissension and are perfect examples of who shouldn't be members of Congress. Sen Rick Scott, as CEO of a chain of hospitals is the infamous corporate criminal responsible for fraudulently billing Medicare/Medicaid over 1 billion dollars making him the single largest health care fraudster in American history. His company was fined over 1 billion dollars but he never went to jail instead he later became Governor of Florida and is currently a US Senator trying to disrupt or dismantle our Social Security system. Since gaining control of the HOR republicans neglectful and cowardly abandonment of responsibility for the interests of the people and their outrageous partisan behavior demonstrates their amenability to a dictatorship which warrants scathing criticism. Since trump left office amid growing political tensions, Republicans who consistently perpetuated heavy government spending under trump suddenly have become hawks on spending only to derail Biden's plans. In June 2023 these hypocritical debt hawks at trump's urging were eagerly prepared to watch the nation default on its debt unless proposed cuts to social programs were adopted.

There's concise and accurate reports of this being their intent which is repulsive, shameful and exclusively harmful to seniors, the disabled and ACA participants. One can reasonably conclude that there's a new radical right wing MAGA mobster party which has metaphorically placed the old GOP on life support and trump signed a do not resuscitate order. House Republicans consciously disregard the consequential irreparable harm a trump 2024 victory would cause and in humiliating fashion have pledged loyalty to their Mara Lago boss over their constitutional oath's reducing themselves from advocates for to impediments against democracy. Rather than engaging in critical electoral initiatives they're operating outside the norms of politics and are fully on board with trump's efforts to kill the Republican party and dismantle our democracy. I understand but can't accept why the trump endorsed incoming 2022 republican congressmen are swayed by this farce perpetrated by trump but why are the senior members of the party so complicit. The harmful impact of the recent bills they're proposing in Congress angers their supporters and has prompted the exodus of many members of the party who have been exposed to the truth. For example. a Florida state senator's proposed bill wants any bloggers writing about the Governor and other members of his executive branch to register with the state or face fines. This nonsense is directly from Putin's play book where you can find that in 2014 Putin signed a law forcing bloggers to register with the Russian media office. This MAGA mobster agenda has a keen interest in Putin's way of ruling and are prepared to replicate it here if trump returns to office or if DeSantis wins.

Without exception republican leadership in both houses of Congress are lap-dogs to trump, who despite having no title other than ex-president, continues to wield smothering influence over them all. HOR republicans consistently exhibit their weakness, cowardice and a lack of courage in the party to oppose trump in spite of the perilous threat he poses. I've thought of how we can derail this partisan runaway train that wants to attack, discredit and dismantle our rule of law, before our way of life is upended.

Many members of Congress are millionaires before or have become millionaires after being elected to office which should prompt questions about their motivation to serve and who are they really serving. What compels those who were rich before their arrival to supposedly set aside their lucrative business interests for a comparably modest congressional annual salary. More likely than not there are corrupt members of Congress who plan and capitalize on ways to enrich themselves and in furtherance of their plans they ignore, reject or even disrupt legitimate legislation favorable to the masses. They actively engage in legalized bribery with donors and consequently participate in insider trading because of insight acquired as members of the legislative body. I must point out that any congressional member of either party who hasn't spoken out, against trump's role in J6th, has failed America, betrayed their oath's and I'm convinced they must be removed from office if this country is to rebound from its spiraling descent. We have too many self-serving people in office and the practical solution is the adoption of term limits for all judiciary and legislative appointments to government and adjust the work calendar for both the SCOTUS and Congress. Currently the Justices are off work from the end of June through October and Congressional sessions are held about 8 months in a year. Reforms should include:

All SCOTUS judges and all federal judges should have what I'd call an 18-72, which is 18 years of service that is capped at age 72 and must retire if either threshold is met.

This proposal should be presented and immediately adopted as an amendment to (article 3 section 1) of the US Constitution. Senator's should be limited to two six year terms and after sitting out one full term can qualify again for an additional six year term.

HOR members serve only five consecutive two year terms and after two cycles out can qualify again for a maximum of three more 2 year terms.

Eliminate the current lifetime pension for House members after three terms and instead require 12 years of consecutive or intermittent service for this benefit.

Adopt a policy increasing the work schedule for both houses of Congress from the current 7 months annually to at least 10 months annually and eliminating any accrued benefits or pension for any member convicted of crime while in office.

100K fine and 5 year imprisonment for any member involved in insider trading.

Criminalization of all lobbyists.

Eliminate corporate and billionaire donations to campaigns/candidates and cap individual donors. Devise a system of equal supplemental state funding of campaigns for primary winners.

This will afford the country an opportunity to cycle in new fresh ideas from less aging members like that found in Jamaal Bowman and 2022 congressman Maxwell Frost. We need new voices in Congress who'll stand against the corporate capture of the government, that's no longer being run by democracy or by politicians, but rather is fueled and being run by corporate donors. While voters may be frustrated with the national legislative process it must be noted that a lot of Republican led state legislatures duplicate on the state level a lot of the absurdities adopted by Congress on the national scale and are in need of a cleansing or a purge of its MAGA members as well. I'll offer a brief glimpse into what has corrupted our current political body status.

Chapter 7

In 1971 FECA (Federal Election Campaign Act) was passed which limited the influence of political action committees (PACs) by adding donor disclosure requirements as well as donor contribution limits. Before further delving into this topic let me parenthetically pause to say we must end the disenfranchisement of anyone criminally charged but yet to be convicted because of much data reflecting that many innocent people are ensnared by false accusations if they can't afford bail they are incarcerated and their ability to vote is suspended. But those accused who can afford bail continue to enjoy voting privileges.

This can fairly be resolved by adopting measures that allows a polling station at all detention facilities for those awaiting trial or convicted of only a misdemeanor. Now, returning to FECA which led to the creation of the media game to skirt FECA compliance because politicians were already addicted to corporate money. PACs started using TV commercials to try and influence elections. A group called Citizens United founded in 1988 brought into politics unlimited campaign contributions and shielded all donor information. Citizens United secretly operates as a front group that funnels money to candidates which consequently causes immeasurable damage to our democracy because its corrupting influence always result in a quid pro quo.

We'll never know the full extent of the damage caused by this form of legal bribery but hope was temporarily found in a 1990 SCOTUS decision that banned corporations from using money to defeat or elect a candidate. SCOTUS would reverse its 1990 decision in 2010 resulting in open season for PACs which now enjoys unlimited campaign spending. In the election cycle of 2021-2022 the top 50 of 100 donors gave over $541 million to democrats and republican received $697 million from their top 50 donors. And we must understand that in Congress a lot of this money comes with expectations and strings attached and when they are not met the donor money ceases and the member becomes less funded and vulnerable in the next election cycle.

For instance a PAC raised over $100 million in 2012 and the top 100 donors made up just 3% of all contributors. But that same 3% of donor's gave 80% of that total $100 million. In 2011 the Montana Supreme Court has ruled that Citizens United will now have to disclose all donor information contradicting the earlier SCOTUS decision. This decision I hope, will increase transparency in our democracy and just might become the catalyst for SCOTUS to revisit the case and bring an end to these big money donors. And please note that this does not include the nearly 3/4 of a billion dollars ($660 million) in foreign lobbyists spending from 2017 thru 2019. We need to repurpose FECA's mission of getting corporate money out of politics because the constitution begins with "we the people" and not with "we corporations."

Since the birth of the nation we've been on an ascending trajectory to economic, military and international power. But I have a pessimistic opinion about the Country's ability to sustain its global position of dominance because of its polarized political environment. American democracy has been fractured by this accelerated political polarization which began inauguration day 2017 and has prompted nationwide social dissension and reversed the trajectory on which it had been. America has been divided against itself by political buffoons whose partisanship prevents any concrete legislation that benefits its citizens from advancing while they engage in these exaggerated cultural war issues.

We don't have to wait on China or Russia to create a conflict that prompts a military response from us because it's been said long ago that if this nation falls it will be from within. Sadly, congressional Republicans, led by Gym Jordan and James Comer, have become accessories to Russian intelligence agents as they're promoting the reports of a Russian asset with a questionable credibility background to substantiate their impeachment efforts of Biden. The scary thing is that Republicans are a bigger threat to our democracy than our foreign adversaries whose strong influence and appalling arrogance has positioned us possibly for another civil war. We've already seen one (formerly outcast Marjorie Greene but now a leader) of the party call for secession of red states from the blue states.

Republican's ideology is one idea and one idea only and that is close down government, whether it's regulation, environmentalism, or support for the basic needs of people. They conveniently ignore the hypocrisy of their party members behavior and attack democrats for the same or less offensive behavior such as Hunter Biden compared to Jared Kushner.

My critique of them is not because I'm a Democrat or that their agenda offends me but rather because they invite and welcome criminals like trump, Gaetz and George Santos into their party and stand in the way of any legislation that would make a difference in the lives of the masses while democrats appear as weaklings allowing this to happen with their milk toast passive resistance. Their party is not only out of order but it's in total disarray primarily because of its unwavering support for trump.

For example student loan forgiveness up to 20K per student was adamantly opposed by Republicans after an analysis revealed that more than 98% of the applicants came from zip codes where the average income is under 75K and about two-thirds were from neighborhoods with an average income below 40K. Because there were more applicants from communities of color than from majority White communities, opposition quickly grew among Republicans. But within this same party there was little or no opposition to bail out banks, bail out airlines or subsidized farmers but when it came to education that's where they drew the line. Too many of the hypocritical Republican congressional members are embroiled in financial conflicts and entanglements but not one is being investigated by the committee that is blindly focused on Biden's son rather than trump, Don Jr, Eric, Kushner, Ivanka, Mnuchin or Santos just to name a few. Four were government employees explicitly engaged in alleged criminal conduct and, with the exception of Santos, have attracted no interest by the committee or law enforcement which is responsible for holding them accountable.

Republicans are turning away from making an analysis of issues and determining its consequences, engaging in traditional debate, brainstorming, or presenting evidence during sessions and have become obstructionist to progress. Democrats in their opposition to this need to forget about decorum and be just as assertive, boisterous and aggressive as the Republicans. All Republicans love pandering to the notion that we have a serious problem at our borders but corporate executives claims of a labor shortage prevents congress from developing a real plan for border security because of corporate interests in cheap labor. Politicians strategically use this issue to pander to a desperate political mass and say elect me and I'll build a wall. Americans are tired of this failing two party political system that can't simultaneously address foreign policy or racial and wealth divides but will boisterously defend tax cuts for the wealthy and resist any reform of gun laws.

Those aged 35 or younger when asked would you rather live in a capitalist or socialist economy the majority said socialism. Most of them didn't know fully what socialism is but because of their understanding and anger with capitalism they know that's not for them. The theme of capitalist is winners (corporations) against losers (workforce) which results in constant social struggle. It's not necessarily what those 35 and younger like rather it's what they don't like that drove their choice of socialism. The level of political battle in the country is fierce. Republican and Democrats attack each other figuratively and literally, you remember January 6th.

Democrats need to develop a new sensitivity to challenges we face such as a health care system that's twice the cost of anywhere in the world, we have the highest income inequality in American history and 4% of the population benefits to the detriment of everybody else. Democrats seem incapable of simply raising taxes on the wealthy who pay little to no taxes compared to the American labor force. For instance from 2017-2018 trump paid hundreds of thousands of dollars in taxes to China while paying the US just $750 in taxes in both 2017 and 2018. This alone should inspire everyone to support a simple change in the tax laws that prevents abuse of the system by the wealthy. Appropriate tax rates for the wealthy and corporations would generate billions in revenue that would not only defray some of the cost of our national debt but also sustain some educational and social programs.

The corporate captured congressional republicans aid and abetment of trump is solely what preserved his presidency through two impeachment trials should be viewed with contempt and disgust. I have noticed a rise in economic populism among Republicans who are deceptively posturing as if they hate corporations while advancing favorable corporate legislation and underhandedly raking in corporate dollars. They're engaging in a magnitude of massive fraud and widespread deception that allows for the termination of all regulations and rules even those found in the constitution. Their public claims of caring for the country, law and order, and their constituents is just an illusion. They don't care that corporations refuse to pay their workers a living wage or that when workers productivity increases, enriching the company, their wages remain stagnant.

This corporate capture of the right wing is maintained by dark money from corporate donors to congressmen on a quid pro quo basis which is simply legalized bribery. What Republicans often refer to as the swamp in DC, exists and thrives because of former congress members, lawyers, former federal agency executives, lobbyists and consultants all leverage their influence on Capitol Hill. Relationships, developed by intersecting interactions are maintained and capitalized on creating the atmosphere for influencing and crafting legislative policies benefitting industries they themselves profit from.

There was a 5 year ban on executive branch officials lobbying the government after leaving the government but trump weakened that ban by saying it applied only to the agency where the former executive worked not the government as a whole. And the spineless Republican congressmen and a few Democrats pretend to have concerns about Corporate America's profit motives but they stay far away from legislating any laws to reign in lobbyists that could affect corporate profit margins. New representation in Congress is necessary across the board because too many have already been contaminated by this brand of corruption and legalized bribery and they can't be trusted to reform themselves.

Lately, the national representatives of our government has been operating peculiarly, as they've been unable to address real problems or move to solve them. What's disappointing but sadly not surprising is trump devalues and disrespect women and proudly takes credit for killing Roe vs Wade. In 2016, he proclaimed that based on his experience as a builder that he was going to build new infrastructure throughout the nation but during his entire term nothing ever happened. Biden got the infrastructure ball rolling by starting one of his first projects in a red state he lost on 2020. Can you imagine the response from Republicans if trump had an infrastructure plan and he started it in a blue state. Some of the petty tactics on the Republican agenda is to own or blame the Libs, misdirection, projection and excuses. These tactics are selectively used based on circumstances or conditions. They love to talk about China being our biggest threat but not one is suggesting that a strategic dialog with China needs to take place in order to avert potential conflict. President Kennedy once said, "Let us never negotiate out of fear but let us never fear to negotiate."

American policy maker's have what I'd refer to as a competition complex when it comes to China. They're horrified and fear China catching up or surpassing us on the global stage especially in economics and technology where China has capable people investing heavily in research and development. Our policy makers have a dangerous perspective, one we should not persist in and that is any China progress, somehow diminishes the US. This political animosity towards China has been brewing since the trump administration and it's time now to negotiate with China, remember Nixon did it. A glimpse of trump's foreign policy shows that besides escalating tensions with China, trump walked out of the Paris climate agreement, walked out of the WHO, walked out of UNESCO, cut aid, behaved atrociously, imposed unilateral sanctions and this does not even include the Civil rights and human rights violations here at home.

Then the Biden administration begins in the shadow of an insurrection and Republicans quickly go to their playbook and blame it all on Biden. I have one burning desire which is to get this book to every trump supporter with the assurance that they'd read and research it and hopefully it results in them turning away from the weird psychopathic former president and together we can begin the work of becoming normal again. We need to relearn the lesson of behaving in a civilized way if we're going to have a civilized relationship with other countries because in this nuclear armed world it would be dangerous to do otherwise. If one were to survey today's global portrait they'd find that our Gross Domestic Product (GDP) which gauges our relative economic power, as a measure of the output of our goods and services over the period of a year. Last year our GDP was 21 trillion dollars with an average annual growth of 2% to 3% over the last 30 years.

Russia's GDP in the most recent year is about 1.5 trillion dollars. Russia is not and never has been an economic competitor with the US, it doesn't come close.

China had a GDP of 17.5 trillion dollars with an average annual growth of 6% to 9% over the last 30 years which makes them very competitive with the US.

I point this out for the readers who perceive Russia as the greatest threat to the US and to clearly illustrate for them with this data why its China instead. You hear a lot of Republicans bashing Ukraine instead Putin's invading army but Putin is not a threat, he's their friend. You ever wonder why trump declared a trade war with China? He imposed sanctions and he applied tariffs in an attempt to stop or reverse China's progress. And now our support of Ukraine against Russia, who is China's most important ally, can lead us and our allies down a path that we really don't want to go down. That's one reason among others why Biden needs to meet with China.

I want to give you a quick quiz. If you had to guess which one of these two groups members, the NBA, or the NFL is being described: 36 have been accused of spousal abuse, 7 have been arrested for fraud, 19 have been accused of writing bad checks, 117 have been bankrupt or bankrupted at least two businesses, 3 have done time for assault, 71 cannot get a credit card due to bad credit rating, 14 have been arrested on drug related charges, 8 have been arrested for shoplifting. 21 are currently defendants in lawsuits 84 have been arrested for drunk driving in the last year and one who we can't say with any certainty who he really is other than he has a seat at the table. (Answer: it's not the NBA or the NFL, it's the USHOR). I can't say for certainty what percentage of them have been corrupted or are being influenced in that direction but if you find 30 untainted out of its 435 members I'd be surprised.

This congressional body through their divisive and despicable support of trump (who cares nothing about democrats or republicans only total power) is complicit at best or instrumental at least in reversing the trajectory of the nation. They've been duped, deceived and lied to by trump and their thirst for power will never be quenched as trump leads them to a desert of political despair. History reveals an identical reversal of a nation's trajectory in Mussolini's rise to dictator in Italy which is relevant as a domestic example for our nation today. He was Prime Minister of a democracy who chipped away press rights and freedoms for three years before being indicted for corruption and to escape he declared dictatorship effectively converting a once democratic society into a fascist one.

If one truly understands trump idolized men like Mussolini, Hitler and Putin then it would be clear what his true goal is. His short-term goal is to win the 2024 election in order to escape his mounting legal woes and from that vantage point he will be able to destroy or disrupt functionality of the government which will position the nation for a takeover by him and his republican congressmen. He projects himself as a strong man and publicly portrays himself as an emblem of national strength which has been effective in establishing his personality cult following. The tools of authoritarianism are violence propaganda, corruption and trump included his own fake masculinity. It's crucial to recognize that in reality trump is weaker than a toy poodle perpetuating a mythical aura of strength and in his perception others are inconsequential.

The constant lying and pandering, to his already frustrated with the government supporters, has enabled him to mask his true character and his aspirational desire in 2024 to seize total control of the government which he came close to doing on January 6th. One seeking to understand trump must realize to him loyalty equates to value and anyone disloyal is disposable. His actions are always driven by self-interest and he has a distorted perception of (self and power) along with a mindset devoid of empathy or conscious which exemplifies his deeply flawed worldview. Listen closely to his critique of others with justifiable skepticism because he repeatedly makes a revealing mistake as most of the time when he talks about others, he's telling you about himself. In 2016 he began his candidacy with micro-aggressive tactics against his opponents which has ballooned to outright attacks against all opposition. But the end for him is nearing and the majority of voters aware of the extent of his criminal conduct, political corruption and moral turpitude will prevent his return to the White House unless it's for a tour through the public visitor's entrance.

We have a dangerous racist MAGA movement in this country instigated as a personality cult that's been prompted and propelled by trump but it goes much deeper. This imitator singlehandedly changed the political culture of the entire Republican party and submitted it to an authoritarian discipline. He failed to go further only because he didn't have adequate time to strategically place supporters in the areas of need. He had elites throughout government agencies collaborating with his efforts, like senator Mike Lee who asked Meadows (trump's chief of staff) how else he could help the leader, in his stolen election claim, besides his already 14 hours a day efforts. It's unclear whether the number of people he placed in these agencies are still on his side.

When trump lost in 2020 it immediately triggered a deep panic within as he realized the potential repercussions of his crimes were on the horizon and that the protection of the office was gone along with any acclaim or immunity. It was like a death to him because he knew that his corruption could now be thoroughly investigated.

But spawned imitators like DeSantis in Florida (the more disciplined extremist) who look at what's working for trump and how he himself can hijack it like a kind of syndrome where he embodies the spirit of trump but less of the baggage. The unfortunate tragedy of it all is that from their offices in the system they can semi-permanently transform the system. For instance DeSantis is banning African American studies in Florida schools and has threatened termination of any non-compliant teachers. This menacing move already has triggered widespread student protests throughout Florida but seemingly to no avail thus far. As the overall racist MAGA movement goes, we shouldn't focus just on the central figure trump. Fascist demagogue Tucker Carlson and his Fox colleagues are prepared to uphold on their network trump or any like-minded replacement. Republican Congressional and gubernatorial enablers are equally prepared to enthusiastically support trump or someone like minded in 2024. For instance, DeSantis has 45 billionaires (many who've shifted their loyalty from trump) backing him giving him a huge war chest for a 2024 bid.

But trump comes from the Russian school of kompromat which is the collection of compromising information on people and threaten to use it for an edge against his opponents. There are many unpublished reports that the few republican senators who voted in the 2nd impeachment trial to convict trump had to wear body armor because of threats and also reports that many senators were literally crying due to stress when going against trump. Trump has been radicalizing his followers since 2015 by promoting violence as a viable option for securing and maintaining power and with his absolute control over a spineless Republican contingent in Congress he can rightfully be perceived as the most dangerous threat to the country.

While unpredictable, no one should be surprised at all about what trump did in promoting January 6th. When he couldn't get the military to support his intention to declare martial law he assembled many cultivated extremist, neo-Nazis, fanatics, skin heads, violent people and militia groups and unleashed them on the Capital because Mike Pence did what his job required of him that day and not what trump wanted him to do. We know there was widespread institutional complicity that day because outnumbered capital police couldn't get the support they needed for hours in spite calls from the House Speaker, DC Mayor and the two bordering state Governor's. There were apparent stand down orders given by the trump administration, suppressing a response from the area National Guard. He couldn't use the military to advance his coup attempt but he was certainly able (for a while at least) to prevent them from stopping it. While the coup was thwarted both tactically and strategically it came too close to succeeding to ever trust trump with the levers of power again.

Chapter 8

In 1973 VP Agnew facing indictment for 39 charges vowed not to resign if indicted. Eleven days later he resigned after pleading guilty to one charge, the others were negotiated away. Facing indictments himself, trump has vowed to continue his run for president even if indicted. I wish not to see trump in jail although he's as worthy a candidate to be there but he has to pay for his years of corrupt dealing and that price should be a total ban from politics and absolute bankruptcy because of his decades of financial crimes. He can live off his government pension which he doesn't deserve. And if the country is to reverse the descending spiral of its trajectory a makeover is needed in state legislatures, the courts, congress and some governors' offices. No president can make or break the country without the assistance of these offices. Optimism says we as a nation can return our country to an ascending trajectory but we must galvanize our economic engine and not focus too much on competing with China's economic position.

China has a population of 1.4 billion and we have about 350 million. With their annual GDP average of 6% to 9% they will eventually surpass the US economically and that will be a testament of their fortitude and developing technology. In this particular matter my criticism is of the US because instead of using this projection as motivation to spur an increase in our annual GDP we look to impose sanctions on China with the hope this will decimate their progress. That's no legitimate reason to make them an enemy or go to war against them. Instead we should adopt a concerted strategy which inspires investment in technology, research and development as well as education because only advances in these areas will allow us to continue to excel and ascend to greater heights than before. And maybe partnering with China in areas of shared interests would dispel any perceived hostilities and be not only good for both nations but the world as well.

Abuse of its citizens has been repeated throughout the history of the United States. The murdering of Native Americans, the enslavement of African Americans, the internment camps for Japanese Americans forcibly sterilized American citizens and the sanctioned lynching of Blacks. There's been an abject failure to represent the unity implied in the country's name and it is based solely on race which has us more divided today than ever. Until this trend is reversed the country will never reach the true height of its potential.

There are several media companies whose refusal to broadcast two factors on their networks (the corrupting impact of dark money in politics and the Republican party's tilt towards fascism) that could enlighten the broader public sparking in our political arena the necessary changes. Fundamentally, the state of the current political landscape is inaccurately reflected in the language most media agencies talk about which fosters both political and social polarization. Despite conflicting widespread news reports that are influencing public perception and adversarial disagreements politically we can develop a bipartisan prodemocracy coalition which preserves and protects democracy by upending trump's 2024 run for president.

History reveals that if Justice is perverted, denied or fails, vengeance is the inevitable recourse. We have a large segment of Republicans who're categorizing themselves as victims of the government and because of their rage are suggesting secession from the union or in some instances alluding to civil war. I have a greater abhorrence of injustice as any other man and find it hypocritical when the perpetrators of injustice claim to be its victim. With an infusion of the MAGA repellent of decency sparked by trump and representing 20% to 25% of the country the spiritual, religious and judicial concepts they once esteemed have devolved into a culture of violence. Just look at two of the weaker gender members of the party Marjorie Greene and Lauren Boebert who both have boisterously made public statements (J6th being their 1776 and making the country Christian only which supports my assertion. And when the men in the party are silent in response to such statements it only infers that they are supportive of such rhetoric. In order to thwart the efforts of a complete takeover by the MAGA movement a displacement mechanism needs to be developed which has to include the adoption of term limits for federal and local offices.

The Maga mobsters whose allegiance to trump have already signaled that they're amenable to a fascist takeover or Civil War. With optimism I must emphasize, that at least 75% of the country is opposed to either of those prospects which is sufficient to thwart either effort. To escape the image of the embarrassing spectacle we've become in the eyes of the world it's important that we move away from the left blaming the right or the right blaming the left and awaken from the slumber of dissension that's pushing the country toward a perilous point.

Make no mistake that my criticism of Republicans throughout this book in no way absolve democrats from scrutiny because many of them also play the game of financial exploration but draw the line at attempting to take over the government. That's why term limits would apply to all appointed or elected public service. The republicans unified and continuing insistence that trump won the 2020 election despite compelling evidence to the contrary is the spearhead of a clear and present danger to the country. It must be remembered by all citizens that the constitution says We the People have the power not we the corporations, or we the billionaire donors or even we the politicians who do by proxy have a degree of our power when they are elected by us. Too many politicians get elected then act as if their constituents surrendered absolute power to them and quickly forget about crafting any legislation beneficial to the masses while quickly exploring ways to enrich themselves. We the People must make our voices heard loud and clear before our system of government is replaced and it's too late. The trajectory that republicans have us on Is adversarial to the social order in the country as they embrace racism, threatens voting rights, undermines the justice system and interferes with women rights.

The US, once a model for developing nations around the world has been catapulted into a mockery by a criminal former president whose influence has regrettably sparked bitter political infighting and consequently hostile division among its citizens. Absent his modicum of decorum for our system of government trump unfortunately was able to commandeer an entire political party to aid in his unsuccessful effort to overthrow our government. With accountability on the horizon in the form of civil and criminal litigation and no longer afforded the protection of the presidency, trump's unprecedented early declaration of his candidacy for 2024 is a desperate attempt to extricate himself from his legal troubles by claiming that now as a candidate the ongoing investigations of him are equal to election interference. Support among his base has been dwindling while his congressional sycophants seek to thwart or obstruct these investigations and surround him with an unwavering and solidified loyalty despite the threat he represents to our democracy. Never before have I witnessed congressional interference in active criminal investigations which is indicative of the control trump has over his fervent network of sycophantic congressmen and should be perceived by the DOJ as an attack on democracy warranting investigations of these obstructionist congressmen.

Since its formation, the 118th Congress's Government weaponization committee has itself been weaponized in an orchestrated effort to interfere with investigations into trump and its chairman has been engaged in Banana Republic level antics by overlooking trump's weaponization of the DOJ and is instead blatantly intervening in both local and federal investigations to protect his corrupt leader. This committee, whose lack of competency is glaringly obvious is led by Gym Jordan who personally obstructed the reports of the sexual abuse of students while assistant coach at Ohio State university.

Now he zealously uses the official power of this committee to prevent, hinder, undermine or disrupt any investigations that would risk exposing trump's crimes. In a campaign of unprecedented harassment and intimidation the committee repeatedly attempted to undermine criminal investigations into trump in both NY and GA. These elected officials would better serve the country, their constituents and fulfill their oath's by doing their congressional jobs and not intruding or interfering in ongoing criminal matters in state courts.

This interference reflected in the activities of the committee indicates the committee was improperly named and that a more appropriate name would be the Committee to Obstruct Justice. Gym Jordan is one of the biggest hypocrites in the 118th Congress who not only ignored sexual misconduct claims made by students he participated in the J6th planning and was without question one of the congressmen being referred to when trump asked his DOJ to just say the election was corrupt and leave the rest to me and the Republican congressmen. While this committee led by Jordan does have limited oversight capacity in federal investigations which never applies to ongoing cases it has absolutely no jurisdictional power to meddle in state or local investigations. Jordan's attempt to have the NYDA appear as a witness is clearly an outrageous attempt to guarantee the total immunity and impunity of a one-man crime wave (trump) and completely elevate him above the law.

The birth of the oxymoronic stop the steal slogan was actually the inception of the start the steal efforts by trump and his cast of deceptive congressional supporters. The climate of mass hysteria fueled by the dissemination of misinformation about the 2020 election originated with trump and gave rise to the visceral powder keg ignited on J6th. As his legal perils mount in the form of civil trials and the pending criminal indictments in desperation, trump's coercive commands for a complicit congressional committee to interfere with NYDA's investigation is reflective of the control he still has over the party.

On 3/21/23, trump's reaction to imminent legal threats was to disgustingly incite and inspire a bomb threat against the NYDA's office following widespread reports of an indictment expected to be announced later that day. I must mention as a reminder that throughout his presidency trump repeatedly has attacked courts, law enforcement officials, judges, public officials and even individual jurors in other matters. This deliberate and traitorous disruption of the functioning of our justice system by trump and representatives of a major political party whose embrace of mercenary like Qanon promoted conspiracy theories is largely responsible for the problems the country faces in 2023.

We as a nation must adopt ways to restrict and then remove those impediment to democracy members already entrenched in the congressional body and prevent like-minded Qanon adherents from becoming members of Congress which I believe will effectively reverse the trajectory the country has been on since trump became president in 2016. During the 2023 CPAC rally all of the speakers including trump proudly stood beneath a banner depicting the group's slogan "We are the Domestic Terrorist." Following that event trump strategically selected Waco, Texas (now considered to be a right-wing shrine) as the site for one of his rallies which coincided with the 30th anniversary of the deadly 51 day standoff of the Branch Davidian cult against the government. The site of the rally and the theme of trump's message were attempts to amplify his anger and create a menacing atmosphere as he did preceding J6th.

A group of MAGA members of Congress led by the willfully stupid Marjorie (the socks stay on) Greene formed a delegation to visit the insurrectionists who tried to dismantle our democracy now being held in the DC Jail. Greene declared she was a victim of the rioters during her 2022 reelection debate but now her prevailing lunacy has her advocating on behalf of the rioters who victimized her. She formed this congressional delegation of members who also were threatened on J6th by this group of riotous terroristic thugs and she now is seeking to not only embrace but to transform them criminals into patriots. In the optics department this raises the question of how is she, not just a member of Congress but a leader in the Republican caucus. The Republicans are adamantly persistent in their support of the rioters as they've previously attempted to visit the jail in the summer of 2022 and were refused access.

Now that they wield power in the HOR they painted a picture of the defendants abuse at the jail in order to gain access to the facility on 3/25/23 and met with the criminals. Activists for decades have been sounding the alarm about inhumane conditions in prisons and Republicans suddenly are interested in the issue because of what they rebranded as political prisoners. These political prisoners as they are now perceived by Republicans are responsible for:

326 are charged with assaulting, resisting or impeding officers.

306 are charged with corruptly obstructing or influencing an official proceeding.

919 are charged with entering or remaining in a restricted federal building.

61 are charged with destruction of government property.

Anyone with a frame of reference for what prisons and jails conditions look like would find that treatment of the rioters at the jail is above par. They're housed single cell and have 12 hour daily access to laptops and tablets affording them communication with family. They have more privileges in DC jail than defendants in any jail across the country. The leaders of the trip were in essence going on a field trip to see their heroes and the defendants got to see their heroes. This same group of congressmen were opposed to Biden's negotiations with Russia for Brittany Griner's release and my sarcasm makes me wonder how long will it be before they schedule a trip to Gitmo. It's very hard to comprehend the depth of depravity these far right wing congressmen will go to spread their disinformation on behalf of the civilly convicted sex offender and criminal ex-president. The January 6th committee investigation established a time-line of trumps actions throughout that day which reflects his neglect, his ineptitude and his total disqualification of him ever holding that office based on the 14th amendment. The following is a chronological catalog of trump's troubling behavior on J6th:

730am- current chairman of a House Committee Jim Gym Jordan has a phone call with trump and afterwards text Meadows saying that VP Pence should be prepared to overthrow the election.

924am- trump calls Jordan continuing to promote the efforts to pressure Pence to overthrow the will of the voters.

955am - SS agents tells trump that the rally on the ellipse has a lot of people armed with weapons.

1015am - SS tells Meadows about the armed people and got no reaction from him.

1047am - Giuliani and Eastman give speeches on the ellipse calling for the overthrow of the election.

1120am - trump continues to pressure Pence calling him a wimp for refusing to go with plan to not certify the election.

1150am - with full knowledge that crowd on the ellipse were armed trump tells his staff to drop the magnetomers at the ellipse.

1200pm - trump speaks at the ellipse and attacks Pence once again.

100pm - Proud Boys break the first line of defense and enter the Capitol.

110pm - trump aimed the ellipse crowd at the Capitol and tells them to go there and he'd be there with them.

119pm - trump goes back to the White House after SS refused to take him to the Capitol.

125pm to around 4pm - trump sat watching on TV, with glee, the events unfolding and did absolutely nothing to end the assault on the Capitol.

2pm - White House general counsel Pat Cipalone ask Meadows to tell trump to stop the riot.

215pm - Cipalone repeats his request to Meadows which is rejected.

224pm - trump sends a tweet slamming Pence but is silent on the violence he's witnessing on TV unfold at the Capitol.

226pm - for his own security Pence is evacuated from the chamber by SS.

228pm Marjorie (the socks stay on) Greene text Meadows to get trump to calm the people which is rejected.

238pm trump tweets, asking the crowd to just stay peaceful. He doesn't say get out of the Capitol or to lay down their arms.

240pm - the Oath keeper's in military formation enter the Capitol.

244pm - Ashley Babbitt is killed by police as she attempts to break through a barrier to get to the senate chamber.

245pm - rioters enter the Senate chamber and the Speaker's office.

253pm Don Jr. tells Meadows that dad has to condemn this right now.

3pm – Jr. again tell Meadows you got to call off the mob but is rejected.

313pm - trump tweets stay peaceful again he remains silent on the brutality and violence of the crowd and he's aware of Babbitt's death and the assaults on police.

315pm - Ivanka calls Meadows and ask dad to do something. Then she tweets to stay peaceful and calls the rioters patriots. Note here is where the reference to the rioters as patriots was coined.

331pm - Hannity of the Fox network text Meadows asking that trump tell the rioters to leave and is rejected.

405pm - Don Jr tells Meadows there needs to be an Oval office address to the crowd right now. He's got to lead now. This is rejected.

417pm - trump finally releases a video telling rioters to go home.

5pm - trump calls Fox host Lou Dobbs to request an appearance on the scheduled 5pm broadcast and is rejected by Fox. After being rejected by Fox, trump tweets: "this is what happens when a sacred landslide election victory is viciously ripped away from people." His day ends when he retires to the sleeping quarters of the White House at 627pm.

This illustrative chronology, reflects the traitorous actions of a president who consistently contrived controversies throughout his term, should afford every voter enough reason to reject him as a candidate for any public office in the country.

His presidency, marred by unprecedented conflicts of interest arising from his decision not to divest from his organization which violated the emoluments clause and netted him over a 160 million dollars from foreign entities. As president he openly trafficked in corruption and criminality and without any exaggeration trump represents the greatest existential threat to the nation and needs to be held accountable for his willful actions and inaction during crises he either created or evaded. A look at the following events which preceded the 2016 election reveal how it was rigged and stolen by trump:

August 2015, Packer, Cohen and trump devised their catch and kill scheme preventing unfavorable reporting of negative information involving trump.

October 2015, doorman at trump towers gets a 30K payoff to silence reports of trump having a child out of wedlock.

June 2016, Karen McDougal gets 150K for silence about extramarital affair with trump.

September 2016, audio of trump and Cohen with both agreeing cash be used for the payoffs.

October 2016, access Hollywood audio comes out on the eve of the election.

October 27, 2016 Stormy Daniels gets paid 130K for her silence.

And the big blunder of FBI director Comey announcing a reopening of the Clinton email investigation two weeks before an election. I believe this one event more than any of those previously mentioned propelled trump to victory in 2016.

All of those actions was for the purpose of being able to influence and win the 2016 election. The misleading claim by trump that the 2020 election was stolen would be appropriately applicable to 2016 because it was stolen by him and the 2020 election could be described as a boisterous attempted robbery of the election by trump.

To better understand what's happening in the country one must look at the history of domestic violence and terrorism in America from the confederate vigilantes, the klux klux klan that advocated lynching and Father Coughlin whose radio broadcasts in the 1930s supported Nazi viewpoints and expressed antisemitic sentiments triggering many attacks on Jews. When Kennedy went to Dallas it was the radical right leaders who championed his assassination and the subsequent assassinations of Medgar, Martin and Bobby.

We're now witnessing with trump something closer to that history which if allowed to persist and go unchecked will derail American Democracy. Since the Republicans refusal to re-authorize and extend the assault weapon ban in 2004 there has been an increase in mass shootings more than tripling the number before the expiration of the ban. Gun related homicide rate is 18 times higher than the average rate of other developed countries. And with over 2K killed or injured in the past 22 years the prevalence of mass shootings in the US compared to the rest of the world is 13 times greater than any other country. Yet our legislators refuses to promote or sponsor any bill that would restrict gun sales or reinstating the assault weapons ban because far too many are in the pockets of gun lobbyists and the NRA.

Every ideologically driven mass killing in the US in 2022 was perpetrated by right wing extremists. States that have less restrictive or more permissive gun laws enjoy more death than states with more restrictive or less permissive gun laws. I do believe every citizen that meets the prerequisites has the right to own a firearm but this right should never include assault weapons of war. Reinstalling the assault weapon ban can be the catalyst which prevents the mass killing of our kids. The obstacle to preventing the necessary change of the law is the fact that the top 20 recipients of gun lobby money in both the house and senate are Republicans who are paid not to care and because of their greed and cowardice they oppose changing gun laws. They have no integrity, cannot be shamed and will never be persuaded but they can be defeated with the ballot which literally is the only remedy.

Instead of introducing legislative reforms members like ex-sex worker and Ted Cruz's alleged former concubine Lauren Boebert, look for ways to increase the risk of gun assaults on the Capitol by advocating for the removal of magnometers from all Capitol entrances and allowing members to be armed on the chambers floor. This foolish incompetent fundamentally ignorant high school dropout Boebert, failed three GED tests before passing the fourth, lacks any intellect and has never read a book but is trying to write one.

In her current position she regrettably is responsible for passing legislation and crafting policy for the nation and has recently called for the elimination of the Dept of Education and for the adoption of a one religion nation Since becoming a HOR member she's been all over the lunacy scale and hasn't introduced or sponsored any bills which is one of the primary function of members of Congress. She laments the welfare system that extricated her mother out of poverty as a former recipient and beneficiary. Her mother could be a poster child for the efficacy of the system Boebert now denigrates by arguing, that while social safety nets are necessary, the US system encourages government dependence. Her uncanny aversion to reality has been repeatedly demonstrated on the house floor when presenting unfavorable data from the trump era and erroneously ascribing it to Biden. What a gross hypocrite she is who can't draft any sensible legislation for congress to contemplate but she can do cartwheels in the hallways of the Capitol with one of her, menace to their community, kids. She's an embarrassment as a congresswoman who was kicked out of a sold-out family themed event for repeatedly vaping after being asked not to and groping her boyfriend's crotch as he groped her breast for an extended period. If she is the best her district in Colorado can find then from a harm reduction standpoint, they should forfeit this congressional seat.

There are questions as to whether Boebert diverted substantial portions of her campaign funds for her personal benefit which amplifies her greed and stupidity. She deceptively refers to the Biden's as a crime family while her family engages in a variety of crimes. Allegations surfaced for the use of campaign funds for her failed business, personal rent and in 2020 she claimed a substantially excessive $22000 driving milage reimbursement from her campaign funds which equates to an unbelievable 39K driving miles for campaign purposes. It takes 26 hours to drive from DC to her home state Colorado which is about 1700 miles. No congressman would repeatedly drive that distance and accumulate the ridiculous 39K miles claimed for travel reimbursement when planes are available.

We have too many clowns like her in office who have no substantive political agenda other than performing for the camera and fraudulently raking in dark money while doing nothing for the people of her own district or the country. The job performance of the 435 HOR members and the 100 Senator's, with exception of a few, is well below standard. A few examples of their ineptitude includes weakening national security, hurting seniors, undermining workers, shipping jobs overseas, raising costs for families, endangering public safety and refusing to raise taxes on the wealthy. In attacking Biden's proposed budget that includes 350 additional border agents, 535 million for border technology and 40 million to fight fentanyl trafficking they countered with a proposal to eliminate funding for 2K border agents which would make the border less safe. Their counterproductive proposal is dangerous and illustrates why personnel changes in Congress are necessary so the work of restoring our democracy can begin as we isolate and insulate the good members from being contaminated by those corrupt and self-serving members who we're trying to eliminate.

The institutions of our democracy are under vicious and unendurable attack from within and our rule of law is in peril. The GOP has abandoned any pretense of operating under the rule of law and with a determined denial of both the J6th riot and a fair 2020 election, have accelerated the faltering of the pillars of our government. It's not an overstatement to say with certainty that in the months ahead both America's democracy and rule of law will be severely tested hopefully not beyond the breaking point. Preservation of our democracy is contingent on opposing and removing all MAGA members of congress which will insure a hopeful democratic future for the country but failing to do so increases the likelihood of an authoritarian future. Fractured alliances among liberals, moderates and progressives in the democratic party must be solidified which can position them to counter the GOP's offensive. Coordinated efforts by democrats to inform and inspire voter participation in elections at all levels state, local and federal is one of the surest ways to remove those self-serving members along with their corrupting influence from among our public servants.

Republican congressional impersonators and their supportive Maga cult members esteem trump with the title of president even as Biden occupies the office. The unfortunate aspect of this is rather than covering him as the fascist traitor that he is the media's orchestrated response covers and glorifies him as if he were still the president. This former president who ignores the courts, the words of the constitution and the outcome of elections he loses is desperately seeking reelection and for the purpose of publicity has masterfully created conflict which has been effective in maintaining his supporters. An incompetent moron humiliated us in the eyes of the world, deviated from the norms of an American president, made the country weaker and degraded our national security all in an effort to become a dictator. Unquestionably, trump perfectly resembles the "antichrist" as described in the scriptures according to:

2 Thessalonians 2:3-4
John 5:43
Rev 13:2, 13:18
Daniel 7:8, 8:12, 8:25, 11:21, 11:38, 9:27
1 John 2:22
2 Cor. 11:14-15
1 Timothy 6:10

Most of trump's accusations against Biden are actual projections and confessions of what he himself has done or will do or wants to do. Broadcast TV networks complicit, outrageous and disgusting acquiescence in its coverage of trump's conspiracy theory filled rallies are hesitant to report things that paints him unflatteringly. If the media recognizes and realize the negative role their gaslighting, lies and distortions have played since 2016 in acclimating a percentage of the nation to the cult of trump they may become amenable to the reform of their networks and start accurately reporting the news about trump. The influential news networks persist in reporting half-truths with its polarizing brand of propaganda which consequently results dissension/division in our society. This stirs the perception among many voters of a loss of political legitimacy, creating instability and dangerously increasing the susceptibility of civil war.

If we begin applying equal standards of justice to all and not excluding an ex-president simply because he's a candidate for office and enforce the law against all violators regardless of wealth, title or influence it can defray the increasing membership of the MAGA cult and it reduces the hostilities against our government and avert the threat of civil war. When MAGA cult leaders are allowed to attack our system of law or threaten its officials not holding them accountable will only normalize, legitimize and further embolden them to continue their polarization of the population.

We the people can thwart these assaults on our democracy but we must acquire a deeper sense of accountability and responsibility and quit categorizing ourselves as victims in the face of this onslaught by the radical right because we have the power to shape the future by our decisions despite our condition. Because of our fundamental interdependence we must unite around the things that bind us together whether we're democrat or republican, left wing or right wing, blue or red state and rural or urban we all want to be respected, connected, protected as prescribed by our human values. I wholly believe we are all bound together by a web of mutuality and that our collective efforts in pursuit to effecting change can accelerate progress but the efforts must begin with the individual. Start by talking to someone. Listen, absorb and understand that the issues of the country's failings on crime, health, wealth and education will only be remedied by the truly unbrought and un-bossed representatives of the people on Capitol Hill and where there are none, it's our duty to place them there.

Those of my generation and beyond are familiar with the term spring cleaning which applied to the seasonal thorough cleaning of one's home. Well we must get to work on cleaning the houses of Congress in every election cycle until all the dirt and stains of corruption is removed and the concept of compromise reintroduced. When we can live up to implied inference in our country's name "United" States by acquiring unity then we'll be positioned to liberate ourselves from the corrupting influences so prevalent in our society. Once we find this solidarity among ourselves I believe that with our intellectual capacity, our resilience, our wealth, and our bravery we'll be prepared to face all of the challenges of this world. The inferential theme of this book is that we the people collectively have the power to thwart the efforts of trump's MAGA movement and protect our democracy.

But the most immediate challenge we face is preventing trump from returning to DC as the Commander in Chief. We know he never divested from his personal business when he became president and he brazenly overcharged his secret service protective detail over three times the market rate to stay at his properties profiting at least 2 million dollars. He also made more than 8 million dollars from foreign countries which includes a few unsavory regimes such as Russia, China and Saudi Arabia which according our intelligence agencies is risky business because of the known tactic of foreign governments attempts to sway members of our government like trump and Sen. Menendez.

Following his loss of the 2020 election and the ensuing trump inspired coup attempt on J6th the GOP has become more radicalized and trump's big lie has fueled new oxygen into the GOP extremists who appear poised to elect a criminal to the presidency. One of the most successful and unprecedented propaganda campaigns in history with a strong emphasis on blatant distortions of facts was trump's big lie which got more than 40 million people to discard the evidence of their eyes and ears and accept his big lie. The political landscape on the Republican side has trump positioned to excel in the 2024 primaries because of the authoritarian discipline style and unified messaging he imposed on the party. And trump has his propagandists, so called news networks (Fox, Newsmax and OAN to name a few), that spew repetitious talking points and simultaneously are authoritarian enforcers for trump.

Fueled by his fiercely vengeful characteristics if trump wins the 2024 election he will pick up where he left off dismantling our democracy and it will happen on an accelerated pace due to his familiarity with metaphorical links of our democracy. It's very astounding that, despite the 35K lies he told while in office and his subsequent actions afterwards,

Republicans uncharacteristically adopted a willful suspension of sentiments which allow them to have no disdain at all for trump. They have no comprehension of the depth of vulnerability in which trump places the country and they contrarily find comfort and ease considering nominating him for 2024. Their 2022 seizure of power in the HOR and their willingness to align that power to trump's bid to escape accountability and win the 2024 election exposes them as dysfunctional and reveals to the world the obstacles they've become.

A key legislative achievement on border security was undermined by trump who influenced republicans to withhold support for the bill while they simultaneously blame democrats for failures at the border. They have profound inability to articulate and legislate policies beneficial to the population but are eager to advocate for trump and corporate tax cuts while opposing worker's unions and are adamantly resistant to calls for gun reform or increasing the minimum wage. These members of Congress have revealed without any doubt that they're adversarial to the constitution and are undoubtedly loyal to trump. Based on the antics of MTG, Gaetz, Gym and Boebert our global adversaries are savoring the dissension among our citizens generated by these polarizing members of Congress. Until they abandon trump and his Maga extremism the diminished reputation of the GOP can never be salvaged or rebuilt.

The far-right wing extremists who are now entrenched in leadership positions in Congress are unraveling the fabric and threads of our democracy and appear to be incapable of moral transformation as they exhibit daily their deceptive and ineffective capacities as leaders which must be met with the strongest resistance we can muster. This book's purpose is not simply to highlight the negative connotations of trump and his Maga cult but to inform readers of who this current breed of republicans really are and I would make it available without cost provided that the readers examine and investigate the accuracy of its content before any judgment or condemnation.

Optimism leads me to believe that after affirming the depictions within this book that the reader will be fueled with a sense of vim and vigor and become active participants rather than passive observers in the fight for our democracy. Only an enlightened, aroused and perhaps angered public opinion can generate the resistance required to stop the implosion of our democracy by those republican imposters. A complacent or neutral response to the country being steered towards Civil War is not an option because if the current course is not aborted, one would then be compelled to choose which side to join. The obvious choice should be for "democracy now" because the last frontier of truth and hope for this country are the people themselves.

This Maga extremists compulsion to co-opt, control and define our lives should out of necessity prompt us to band together and repair the tattered threads of our democracy. Above all in our collective pursuit of solutions to our problems we cannot see each other as the enemy. This is not the sentimentality of optimistic idealism but rather a reminder that our polarizing and disparaging feelings resulting from a long conditioning process must be broken which will preferably allow us work intelligently to solve our problems. I hope that those who are not in agreement in this matter will not assume a hostile posture and discount all of the other points in this book because its intent is not to foment consternation nor prompt the formation of opposing camps.

The Maga extremists compulsion to upend American Democracy are far outnumbered by the lovers and protectors of democracy who are determined to penetrate the web of MAGA ignorance which imprisons too many minds and enthralls them in a state of gullible complacency. I offer the readers the following cautionary warning: in pursuit of his most paramount virtue "power" as leader of the MAGA movement trump is determined to penetrate the foundational and institutional fabric of our democracy and is steadfastly determined to destroy it and adopt an authoritarian model in its place. His promulgation of lies and conspiracy theories sows doubt in the minds of Americans who then doubt the veracity and validity of our elections is a dangerous, despicable and desperate tactic to regain the White House.

Republican indulgence in incendiary rhetoric is totally responsible for the tattered fabric of our democracy and the polarization of our citizens and the only way to position ourselves on a path to restoration is the elimination of every Maga remnant from Congress. This begins at the polls in every state, local and federal election until the old republican party is resurrected or preferably a new second party is found. The current republican congressional caucus is at a minimum 85% contaminated by dark money and Maga ideology and it will require their removal and replacement for the party to ever be restored. And all new members to the party, for the purpose of insulation will need to be isolated in order to prevent any contamination from the delusional fascist Maga ideology and dark money influence.

The way it works now is legalized bribery by corporate donors and the wealthy which occurs among congressional members and triggers a deviation from their congressional duties. Among themselves there's a deeply entrenched process that's known as "under the dome strategy" in which the donors and the wealthy bypasses the normal legislative process in order to get their interests and projects through Congress. While it may take a little time the good news is that by voting we the people have the ability to correct these flaws and preserve our Democracy but the nightmare scenario is that failure to do so ensures the demise of democracy and the installation of authoritarianism or fascism in its place. I could have never envisioned in my lifetime that the Republican caucus whether inadvertent or intentional in addition to 40% of republican voters would openly and proudly promote a, criminal and his social ponzi scheme called MAGA, as their candidate for president in 2024.

I'm confounded by their selective gullibility as most of them have some level of higher education which only highlights the fact that degrees on your wall do not certify one as immunized from stupidity. In fact most of their degrees are nothing but paper testimony to the elaborate cost of verified ignorance. This malignant extremist threat to democracy found among the obstructionist republican congressmen and a staggering number of the general public, without question reveals how unrecognizable trump has made the party in his desperate quest for power. There remains an opportunity for the republican party to bounce back from the negative image they've adorned as trump sycophants but the first step in that direction is to sound the alarm to all voters that the country can never allow trump into any public office.

Chapter 9

Throughout this book in spite of my criticism of the political malpractice of the Republican party which appears bereft of any decency and by complicity is responsible for the fractured condition of our democracy, I've repeatedly highlighted some of the dangers we as citizens would incur with a trump return to the White House such as an increase of immoral White nationalists sentiments and the normalization of intolerant language and conduct within his administration which will only embolden his Maga cult and further polarize the country. We can't afford to ignore or dismiss the warnings we are receiving daily through trump's constant assertions alluding to his dictatorial aspirations. We may find ourselves sleepwalking into a dictatorship if we don't prevent trump from returning to the White House in 2024.

The Maga adherents need to start believing their eyes instead of trump's lies. In order to persevere in the preservation of democracy, tactically our antagonistic opposition to trump and his Maga movement must be constantly voiced and our broadcast journalists, rather than avoiding coverage of the outlandish positions of trump, need to start accurately reporting the undisguised detrimental plans trump has for the country. With this course of action I sincerely believe more of the MAGA adherents will abandon the movement in droves as they come to realize that they've been lied to, grifted out of their money through their political donations and that they'll realize the sanity they've ascribed to the movement has revealed itself as utter lunacy.

I remain optimistic that their Maga inspired threat against the country will be surmounted and the diverse preservers of our democracy will prevail. As an incurable optimist I believe that our common good and the collective efforts of the majority population at the election booth will be sufficient to eventually remove all remnants of the deeply entrenched, greedy, corrupt power thirsty congressional republicans who've aligned themselves with trump's Maga cult. Democrats, sane Republicans and Independents in solidarity must work to ensure trump and his appalling congressional enablers who've collaborated with him despite his unending organized criminality, are all defeated. Subsequently, this will at best, position the country to ascend to new heights, or at least restore our semblance of unity that was trampled all over during trump's administration. Eradicating this threat to the country and triggering a reversal of the descending trajectory of our democracy which trump's MAGA movement placed us on should be the immediate priority on America's agenda.

From the sentiments expressed throughout this book one can reasonably conclude that I'm obsessed with a distasteful opinion of trump and if you happen to be among that crowd I hope you'd have an equal disdain. Based on the threat trump represents to the country I can't perceive having any contrary opinion of him and regret that I don't have a broader platform to enlighten those who remain misinformed about him. I'm north of sixty years old and in my lifetime never has the country been attacked from within until J6th and a continuation of that attack is pending that's contingent on a 2024 trump victory.

My suggestion to the readers, who are currently comfortable with our democracy and aspires to protect and improve it, is to not take for granted that everyone is aware of the threat that trump represents but to inform every voter you know how critical the 2024 election is. I would strongly urge that, for political news and views to tune out Fox's propaganda network which strongly supports trump and suppresses factual reporting about him while inaccurately ascribing to him favorable traits he doesn't possess and ignoring his repetitive lies and threats. Sometimes I watch Fox's broadcasts to see what new propaganda they're peddling but I rely on more credible sources like the Meidas Touch, Glenn Kirshner and Brian Tyler Cohen for more accurate reporting. My observations and opinions are intended to provoke people's conscious to understand how serious the situation we're facing. I hope my opinions informs and encourages readers to participate in the 2024 election cycle and to warn of the impending doom if we get it wrong.

My disdain for trump is based on his hypocrisy, the thievery and cheating he's done in his business endeavors, his promoting of the structural erosion of democracy in America, his ineptitude and irrationality as president, his ceaseless lying and prejudices against both minorities and women and the defaming of his rivals. He has been a polarizing figure and intensely controversial throughout his presidency yet despite being plagued with numerous distasteful characteristics he has solidified his grip on the Republican party and is taking them on a reckless legislative joyride as he remains their republican nominee for 2024. This should intensify our motivation to ensure that trump's 2024 campaign is either a sinking ship or one not seaworthy, by simply participating in the VOTE to prevent him from implementing his dictatorial tendencies from the White House. His grip and influence on the party already affords him an ability, from his Mara Lago residence, to prevent border security and aid to Ukraine legislation crafted in the senate from reaching the house for a vote.

What more need I say than to you I have said regarding the importance of Americans collaboratively removing the trump induced polarizing dissension growing in the country and working together to reshape the political landscape while enhancing the lives of the American people. It's a patriotic imperative to participate in 2024 election, as a scathing dismissive gesture to the radicalized Maga extremists and to prevent further erosion of a salvageable democracy that's currently in decline. I profoundly assert our democracy needs to be improved because historically, through either government sanction or church sponsorship it has consistently been adversarial to Blacks due to White power and White fear despite legislated prohibitions. In the Maga world the marginalized will forever be doomed to the margins so they must be made aware that preserving our democracy or simply maintaining it is not in the plans of the habitual liar trump. His unquenchable thirst for power and revenge paired with his affection for violence will resoundingly decimate it and ensure their marginalization.

Faced with this overwhelmingly divisive predicament we need be involved and committed to fight the trump led attempted conservative takeover of our country which requires unity of the entire voting bloc. Due to his susceptibility to cheat, a coalitional only turnout in 2024 will be insufficient to defeat trump despite the disdain of that coalition. If one is viscerally and adamantly opposed to fascism then integrity not party affiliation should motivate voting preferences in 2024 because of the dangers we face if we get it wrong. The defeat of trump in requires the consolidated efforts of liberals, swing voters conservatives and Independents to defeat trump because the undermining of all voters health, wealth, security and freedom are on the ballot. It's past time that we formulate a strategy to reverse the trend where 86% of politicians have a mere 14% to 20% approval rating but manage to enjoy a 97% reelection rate that corporate and billionaire donors engineer. We who are dedicated to the protection, preservation and defense of democracy can't allow this trend to continue. It will only be broken after we are properly informed of our choices and in solidarity realize that the value of our vote is greater than donor dollars.

As I survey the political and social conditions of the nation today I am compelled and challenged to speak specifically about the many complex and complicated problems which I believe can be the catalyst for the utilization of our creative energies working together for the amelioration of the human condition. I refuse to believe that the small group of MAGA menaces which aspires for an inevitable fascist takeover of the country can defeat the morale of the majority of We the People, that stands in opposition to such aspirations. Only the collective use of our vote, talents and abilities can produce a better nation in which to live.

We the people have in our grasp and grip the wherewithal to turn the nation on the right path as the preamble of the constitution reminds us that ours is a government of the people, by the people and for the people. That's why we must rise up in righteous indignation and demand those corporate captured congressmen to start moving in another direction away from their big donors because we know he who pays the piper calls the tune. We're tired of the oppressive conservative forces in politics with their outdated repressive views of minorities while supposedly making decisions on behalf of those minorities when at best they belong on the fringes of the political system until we remove them.

Despite the inherent racism in the bloodstream of America if we unite and mature both psychologically and socially we can begin carrying out the espousal of equalitarian principles throughout the nation. This lofty ambition can never be realized if we allow fear or complacency to immobilize us and as long as the status quo is allowed to continue along the traditional, historical and prejudicial lines of the past which retards cohesion among those minority segments adversely impacted by inequality. It has become necessary for the majority of congressmen, currently part of what constitutes a national leadership team but have no commitment or concern for the people until the next voting cycle, to be voted out of office.

Many are frauds who've been in office for decades having never proposed a bill, offer no input on how to infuse the circulation of the bloodstream of the nation, lack integrity and are totally inept serving their constituents. The psychological reluctance to change has led them into comfortable complacency which diverts them from pursuing a redirection of the priorities of the nation until it becomes a haven for all of its citizens. In conclusion, my blatant criticism and critique of the current congressional republican congressmen does not absolve some democrats who are equally deserving of criticism. But my disdain and disenchantment expressed in this book focuses specifically on republicans because of the immediate imminent danger that party represents to the nation. As we strive to carve out our place in society with different aspirations and different pursuits we must remember along the way to develop a common concern for our fellow human beings because true brotherhood of man is one step after the fatherhood of God.

About the Author

DC native currently residing in Gaithersburg, MD. Retired from Montgomery County Department of Transportation. Former volunteer at DC Department of Corrections for two decades as prison minister until relocating to MD. Presently volunteering as a prison minister at MD Department of Public Safety in Hagerstown. MD.